HOW TO AVOID SIX FATAL LEGAL MISTAKES THAT CRUSH SMALL BUSINESS OWNERS

TONY T. LIU

Your Chief Legal Counsel

About the Author

My name is Tony Liu, and I am a business litigation attorney in Orange County, California. Since 2003 I have focused my practice on helping small business owners both in and outside the courtroom.

A big part of my job is educating my clients, which is why I wrote this book. The best clients are educated clients, it makes their lives and my life easier. I help people owning or running a business avoid legal problems or deal with them the best way possible when they occur.

I hope this book can help you and if you need more than a book, feel free to contact my office.

FOCUS LAW - (714) 415-2007

WEBSITE: www.FocusLawLA.com

BLOG: www.orangecountybusinessattorneyblog.com

LINKEDIN: https://www.linkedin.com/in/tony-t-liu-business-trial-attorney-74214bb/

FACEBOOK: https://www.facebook.com/Focus-Law-141950989865721/

Disclaimer No. 1

The information contained in this video or webinar is for providing general information and does not constitute legal advice or opinion, nor is it a substitute for the professional judgment of an attorney. Thus, before you act or rely on any information provided by this video, you should speak directly with an attorney. Tony T. Liu, a professional law corporation, doing business as, the Focus Law (hereinafter "the Firm"), disclaims all liability for actions taken or not taken based on the information on this video or webinar.

Disclaimer No. 2

Furthermore, no attorney-client relationship can be created from the use of this video or webinar. Neither your receipt of information from this video or webinar, nor your use of this video or webinar to contact the Firm or one of its lawyers, creates an attorney-client relationship between you and the Firm. You will become a client of the Firm only when you sign an engagement agreement (setting forth the scope of the Firm's engagement, the fee arrangement, and other relevant matters), and pay the fees as required. As a matter of policy, the Firm does not accept a new client without first investigating for possible conflicts of interest (for example, the Firm may already represent another party involved in your matter) and obtaining a signed engagement letter.

Table of Contents

Introduction

Although I have been successful and won many cases at trial for my clients, many times I just have not felt quite right.

After the judge announced the verdict in my clients' favor they didn't jump up and down, give me a high five, and say, "Hey. We won the case! Good job, Tony!" Instead, I always hear, "Yes!" They sound as if pressure is being released or a burden was just lifted from their shoulders, which emotionally and legally is true. But not necessarily financially.

When I present the final bill to my clients, and they see exactly how much they spent on their litigation, most nod their heads, acknowledge the cost, accept it with gratitude and honor the invoices. However, their responses are sometimes inconsistent with the case results I achieved for them.

In United States alone, 20 million civil cases are filed each year, 60% of these 20 million civil cases (12 million cases) are contract disputes and 75% are employment related. All these cases involve business owners. This is a problem that small business owners must address.

The cost to start filing a case is $54,000. The median cost of a lawsuit is $91,000 (almost $100,000). When the starting litigation cost is multiplied by 12 million (the number of contract disputes per year in the U.S.) it comes to $648 billion dollars being spent each year to start these cases. If these 12 million cases are multiplied by the median cost of litigation ($91,000), the figure is $1.092 trillion. Even with these rough estimates, clearly a significant amount of money is spent each year to resolve contract disputes.

The purpose of this book is to discuss ways small business owners can minimize their risk and exposure to litigation. If a business,

- Is proactive in its management and maintains an awareness of the law, it may still encounter lawsuits but there are strategies that can help minimize the chances that will be sued or need to sue someone else to pursue a contract claim.

- Must file a lawsuit as a last resort, then its management will be confident in a cost effective, positive outcome due to the preparation that was done beforehand.

My approach is to have my clients win the battle before it happens. By planning ahead, being proactive and smart, investments in time, energy and money up front, before problems explode into crises, can yield outstanding returns.

This type of approach is just common sense and you do it every day, you just may not realize that preventative steps can be critical to helping your business.

- Do you change the oil in your car, or not bother and buy a new car after your engine seizes?

- Would you replace a roof that's old and worn or wait to do so after there are water leaks that damage your ceilings and walls?

- Do you maintain production equipment you need for your business or just fix them after they break, hope you have the necessary parts on hand, pay your employees overtime to fix it and deal with angry customers because you're not delivering on time?

This book is about the six legal mistakes that you as a business owner should avoid to prevent getting involved in costly lawsuits. If you do end up involved in litigation, the actions I suggest may help your case and reduce the cost in time, energy and money.

Mistake No. 1
Not Protecting Yourself

If you own a business you're probably pouring your blood, sweat, tears, time, energy and money into it. Because of the time you've invested in your business you're spending a lot of time away from your family and friends. Money spent on your business is money not spent having fun, your family, going on vacation or set aside for your retirement.

Owning a business is a risk and the more you put into it the greater your risk. Doesn't it make sense to limit that risk as much as possible? Shouldn't you take steps to prevent as much financial harm to you, your family and business in case things don't go according to plan?

Protect Your Personal Assets

The first legal mistake I've seen during my practice is business owners conduct transactions under their own names. An individual has a big idea about how to make money and grow a business. The person goes out and implements the idea without much planning in advance. It might be as simple as it sounds, but it often is more complicated in today's business environment.

The biggest reason you shouldn't conduct business under your name is that you need a legal and financial shield between you and your business. This shield,

- Is very important because it keeps your business' debts separate from your personal finances so you are not liable for these debts.

- Can prevent your business' creditors from getting access to your personal assets in case you need to walk away from your business or things don't work out as planned.

This protection is the number one reason to set up a business entity whenever business is conducted. Some of my clients even set up a different business entity for each major transaction.

Talk to your legal advisor about how to protect your assets. If you are in California, you are welcome to call our office and we will provide you with in-depth solutions for your situation.

Perception of Limitations

There are also practical reasons to set up a business entity. It will help you attract resources and clients. If you are conducting business under your name, others may think,

- Your business is just a simple mom-and-pop operation.

- You're a small operator and your business is not scalable.

- You're turning your hobby into something that's not a real business. It's just a side gig.

Although those assumptions may be false, they are common perceptions about individuals conducting business under their own names. If an individual incorporates a business or sets up a limited liability company (LLC) they are perceived to be more serious entrepreneurs.

- They have plans, are more organized and intend to scale their businesses.

- The owners are creating this business for the long term, they are systemized.

- These business owners do not do the work themselves. They have employees.

This step is very important, especially if you want to borrow money from a bank. If the bank knows that you are conducting business under your individual name, it will treat your case as if you, personally, are borrowing the money.

The bank will most likely deny your business loan unless you have collateral or a significant amount of money in the bank. If you have a significant amount of money in your bank account, you may not need a loan from the bank. It's a Catch 22.

If you approach investors to invest in your company, (you want someone to invest $250,000 or $500,000 for a 20% stake in your company), they want to know that your business is serious and scalable. If you don't incorporate your business, deciding to operate as a sole proprietor under your personal name, it's unlikely that investors will invest in your company. They,

- Want to know that their investment will be profitable,
- Expect a certain rate of return on their money, and,
- Seek investments that they can liquidate if they have a conflict with the business owner, you.

This is difficult to do with sole proprietors.

Incorporation has many benefits and comes in three major categories: corporations, LLC's and partnerships. Partnerships are somewhat uncommon today and are gradually being replaced by LLC's so I will not focus on partnerships.

Corporations are creatures of state laws. The laws and regulations concerning them are based on the idea that businesses can flourish and thrive if there's a legal disconnection between the company and its owners. Instead of risking one's personal assets to help a company grow, shareholders may be more willing to accept risk and debt, which may be critical to a business surviving.

A basic tent of American corporate law is that the corporation and its shareholders are different entities under the law. A shareholder, by owning shares, doesn't own the corporation's assets or its subsidiaries nor is he or she liable for its debts or obligations (assuming the applicable laws have been followed).

Other Benefits of Forming a Corporation or LLC.

Corporations and LLC's can exist even if the founding owner dies or sells the business or management changes, as long as all the legal requirements are met. Sole proprietorships and partnerships just end if an owner dies or leaves the business.

Think of a corporation as a separate artificial person (with limited rights and privileges). When you incorporate a business or form an LLC you're essentially creating a separate entity making the business separate from the owner. As a separate, legally distinct entity, the corporation or LLC exists independent from the shareholders/owners and its employees. No matter what happens to the shareholders, directors or employees, the entity itself continues to exist in perpetuity until a time the directors and shareholders decide to dissolve a corporation or they fail to comply with legal requirements.

In a sole proprietorship or general partnership, the owner is the business, what impacts the owner probably affects the business. If there's a personal debt or liability of an owner or partner it can allows a creditor to use the business assets to pay it off whether or not the debt or liability has any relation to the business itself. Personal bankruptcy by an owner or partner will directly impact a business because its assets can be available to any creditors the owner or partner is indebted to.

By incorporating a business or forming an LLC the personal finances of an owner or partner remains separate from the finances of the entity, allowing it to continue without disruption. If an owner becomes incapacitated or dies, a business is normally dissolved unless it can be passed on or sold to someone else. This can be avoided by incorporating the business as a separate entity.

A business owner or partner at some point may want to leave the business or may be forced to leave because of personal or health reasons. Whatever the reason, incorporation allows the free transferability of interest from one person to another. Normally in a partnership with a written agreement, one partner can't transfer his/her interest to another person without the agreement of the other partners. If a partner decides to leave contrary to the will of the other partners, the partnership is automatically dissolved.

Incorporating a business removes this problem by allowing shareholders/owners to freely transfer his or her interest to another without the unanimous consent of all other shareholders. If those starting the business want restrictions against transferring shares and want to control how a shareholder may transfer his or her interest and to whom, that can be part of a shareholder agreement. Unlike a partnership, incorporation prevents a minority shareholder from dissolving a business without cause.

Choices-LLC or Inc.?

The two most common types of business entities are corporations and LLC's. You may ask, "What happened with the C and S corporations?"

These distinctions are primarily relevant to the IRS when a tax return is filed because they have different tax treatment. The differences are subtle, so consult with a CPA to learn the different tax treatments.

These entities also have specific requirements. For our purposes a corporation is a corporation and a C and S corporation are not distinguished.

Many people ask me which business type to choose, an S corporation or a limited liability company (LLC)?

For legal and financial protection you should set up a shield between you and your business. Although there are a few differences in the state laws that govern the different types of businesses, all business types are virtually the same with regard to protection.

If you're forming a new business you can get bogged down in trying to sort out the differences between an S corporation and an LLC. When deciding which is the right one for you and your business you need to decide your priorities. Before you get that far, who will decide those priorities?

The owners of the business will. How many owners of this new entity ("shareholders" for an S corporation and "members" for a LLC) will there be? If there's just one or two of you making these decisions should be relatively easy.

It can be a problem if there are several people involved. Each party may have different views on what should be key priorities for the business. They should come together and rank their priorities and choose the entity which best meets as many of the goals of the parties with the least compromises as possible.

If the parties can't reach a compromise on these basic issues it's best to know this sooner than later. This way a party or two can go their own way before serious disagreements erupt after the business starts.

Possible goals include,

- Limiting potential personal liability to the owners of the liabilities that will come with the business,

- The formalities required for maintaining that limited liability,

- Limiting potential taxes from the business, and,

- Other issues in your particular situation.

S Corporations

An S corporation is a legal entity limiting the potential personal liability of the owners if the entity is properly formed and maintained.

You don't want to create an S corporation with fill in the blank forms found on the internet. If you do there's a good chance the corporation won't be properly formed. You may get the stamped Articles of Incorporation from the Secretary of State but without the necessary follow up with the other documents or formalities required under California law your corporation was improperly formed. If this happens you have exposed yourself to liability because in the future if someone sues you they may be able to "pierce the corporate veil" (see below).

An S corporation requires certain formalities which are generally greater than that of an LLC. To try to maintain personal protection from liability,

- The corporation should properly notice, hold and document annual meetings of the shareholders and directors, as well as any special meetings of the board of directors needed to authorize and affirm certain corporate acts,

- All documents required under applicable law should be filed on time,

- The corporation should be funded with a sufficient amount of capital,

- The corporate secretary should keep the corporation's corporate minute book in order and up to date. The required parties should sign all documents where the corporation is a party, in their capacity as an officer or authorized agent of the corporation, and

- Corporate funds should not be mixed with a shareholder's personal funds.

There are differences in tax treatment between an S corporation and an LLC. Before finally deciding which business, entity is right for you, consult with your accountant.

- An S corporation normally doesn't pay federal income taxes. Its income or losses are divided among and passed through to the shareholders based on their ownership interest. The shareholders must report the income or loss on their own, individual income tax returns.

- The S corporation must pay the California state franchise tax but it avoids the gross receipts tax of an LLC, in which gross receipts of an LLC more than $250,000 are taxed.

- If an S corporation is formed the self-employment tax might be avoided.

For a corporation to be eligible for S status there are fairly strict shareholder requirements.

- There can be no more than a hundred shareholders.
- Shareholders must be U.S. citizens or legal residents, a specified type of qualified trust or estate, but not another corporation.
- Share ownership is shown by stock certificates issued to each party as part of the corporate formation.
- Normally significant changes in share ownership are memorialized in a stock purchase agreement, asset purchase agreement, or other forms of acquisition or transfer documents.
- There can only be one class of stock.

S corporations are managed by the directors, officers and shareholders.

- Shareholders elect the board of directors but otherwise have no right to engage in the daily management of the entity, unless a shareholder is elected as a director or appointed as an officer.
- S corporations are managed overall by the board of directors, who appoint officers to run the daily business operations.

- The officers (a president, secretary and treasurer) are agents for the corporation and their decisions can bind the corporation.

Ownership of an S corporation is evidenced by stock certificates, which need to be issued to each shareholder as part of the corporate formation. If there are significant changes in corporate ownership they are memorialized in a stock purchase agreement, asset purchase agreement, or some other form of acquisition or transfer documents. If stocks (or shares) are transferred, corporate documents need to be reviewed to see if the other party is bound by a shareholder agreement (or a buy-sell agreement) which can limit the transfer of stocks.

Limited Liability Company

To form a California limited liability company the owners (or members) must,

- File articles of organization with the state,

- Agree on key business points to be outlined in a company operating agreement,

- File a Statement of Information with the California Secretary of State, and

- Meet other requirements.

As with corporate formation fill in the blank forms to create an LLC are for those who are penny wise and pound foolish. Often required documents and forms filled out by these consumers are not filed properly and, under the law, as a result, there actually is no LLC. If there is a future lawsuit against the business or a dispute among members this lack of formality and foresight can be a major problem.

A California LLC has more relaxed legal requirements compared to an S corporation. Though member meetings are not required, you should properly notice, hold and document them to help bolster the personal limited liability protection an LLC affords.

For federal income tax purposes, an LLC is a flow through entity. Depending on elections made by the LLC and the number of members, the IRS will treat an LLC either as a S corporation, partnership or as part of the owner's tax return.

- An LLC with at least two members is classified as a partnership for federal income tax purposes unless it affirmatively elects to be treated as a S corporation.

- For an LLC with one member its income, deductions, gains, losses and credits are reported on the owner's income tax return. It can also elect to be treated as a S corporation.

Compared to a S corporation an LLC is more flexible with respect to management and control. In an LLC management and control is with the members (a "member managed LLC") or with the managers (a "manager managed LLC").

The difference is that in a member managed LLC each member is authorized as an agent to bind the LLC because of their membership, while in a manager managed LLC there is a centralized management committee in the form of managers, who may or may not also be members.

The transfer of a membership can be done easily if it's not prevented or limited in an operating agreement or a membership interest buy sell agreement. Before the transfer of an LLC membership interest, these agreements, if any, need to be reviewed.

Incorporating can help you better manage your income. Though you may not be making much money if you just started your business as time passes and you become more successful, you may want to separate your business income from your personal income and take a salary. Forming a corporation allows you to do this. You can leave profits in the business and pay yourself a salary in an amount that's only what you want or need.

Both corporations and LLC's may deduct normal business expenses, including salaries, before they allocate income to owners.

Which business entity is right for you? Only you and any others involved in the ownership in your business can decide, with the help of a business attorney and your accountant.

Conflicts of Interest

Corporate board members need to be chosen when the entity forms. This shouldn't be taken lightly. Don't just name a friend who owns a business or a cousin you like. Board members can have a tremendous, beneficial impact on a company. If they have the company's best interests at heart and have relevant but diverse backgrounds their input can help guide a company through tough times into much better times. That's a difficult task if a board member has a serious conflict of interest problem making the person unsuitable for the board or limit what he or she should or shouldn't do.

A conflict of interest is a transaction or arrangement that benefits an officer, board member or employee on a personal level. Board members may be related to employees, other board members and dual capacity individuals (someone who's an employee and is on the board). He or she may have connection to a competitor or potential competitor. Every board member has a fiduciary duty (a legal obligation to be loyal, truthful, honest and not act to benefit one's personal interest) to the corporation to act in its bests interests and not use his or her access to benefit a competitor or themselves.

Transparency is needed when corporate boards discuss issues and make important decisions.

- Board members need to be able to identify conflicts of interest and disclose them so decisions can be made as to whether the person should remain a board member or simply be excluded from discussion and decisions on a particular matter.

- This level of transparency makes board members more confident about their decisions and should generate more confidence by outsiders concerning the corporation.

Potential conflicts include a board member,

- Being associated with a company that does business with the corporation or is associated with a competitor.

- Uses the information he or she has obtained to personally benefit from starting a new, competing company, or joining an existing competitor.

When deciding who should be a part of a corporate board a potential conflict of interest is an important issue to consider, though not the only one.

No "Get Out of Jail Free" Card

You want to protect yourself and have your business be taken seriously so you incorporated it. But the paperwork is no get out of jail free card if you try to play fast and loose with the law or if you're sloppy when it comes to legal formalities. You may lose the legal protections that come with incorporation or an LLC if another party goes to court and successfully "pierces the corporate veil" and pins liability on you, other shareholders, LLC members or related business entities.

These types of cases aren't common but they do occur. Research by Prof. Eric L. Talley, PhD, JD, of the University of California's Center in Law, Business and the Economy found that of reported California judicial decisions in 2010 the corporate veil was pierced,

- A little over half of the time, but,

- That differed with the area of law: contract, tort and statutory enforcement cases saw it happen half the time but it increases to 65% in criminal prosecutions.

Under California law, as interpreted by the Court of Appeals of California, Fourth District, Division Three in Curci Investments v. Baldwin,

- Normally a corporation is considered a separate legal entity, apart from stockholders, officers and directors, with separate and distinct liabilities and obligations.

- That legal separation can be disregarded by a court if a corporation or LLC is used by one or more individuals or another business entity to perpetrate a fraud, circumvent a statute, or accomplish some other wrongful or inequitable purpose.

- The burden of establishing the veil should be pierced is on the plaintiff.

- Courts normally respect the separation of individuals and corporations. Finding the corporation is just a sham "alter ego" for individuals or another entity is an extreme remedy, to be sparingly used by the courts.

- If these situations are found the actions of the corporation or LLC will be considered to be those of the persons or organizations actually controlling the corporation, usually the shareholders.

- This "alter ego doctrine" prevents individuals or other corporations from misusing the corporate laws by setting up a sham corporate entity formed for the purpose of committing fraud or other wrongdoing.

- The basic question facing a judge is whether finding one entity an "alter ego" of another entity or a person is whether it's fair and equitable given the facts and applicable law.

- Before a California judge can use alter ego doctrine to separate a legal entity from individuals or other related entities, two conditions generally must be met.

1. There must be a sufficient common interest and ownership between the corporation and its shareholders that the separate personalities of the corporation and the shareholder do not, in reality, exist.

2. There needs to be an inequitable (or unfair) result if the acts in question are treated as those of the corporation alone.

Over the years California courts have developed a list of factors that can be considered when making these determinations. There is no formula set in stone. The result in a particular situation should be decided on its unique circumstances. Those factors include, according to the Court of Appeal, First District, First Division, in Associated Vendors v. Oakland Meats,

- Commingling of personal funds and other assets,
- Failure to segregate funds of the separate entities,
- Unauthorized diversion of corporate funds or assets to other than corporate uses,
- Treatment by an individual of corporate assets as his own,
- Failure to obtain authority to issue stock,
- An individual holds himself out as personally liable for the debts of the corporation,
- Failure to maintain minutes or adequate corporate records,
- Confusion of the records of the separate entities,
- Identical equitable ownership in the two entities,
- Equitable owners dominating and controlling two entities,
- The same directors and officers responsible for the supervision and management of different entities,

- Sole ownership of all of the stock in a corporation by one individual or the members of a family,
- Use of the same office or business location,
- Employment of the same employees and/or attorney,
- Failure to adequately capitalize a corporation,
- Use of the corporation as mere shell, instrumentality or conduit for a single venture/business of an individual or another corporation,
- Concealment and misrepresentation of the identity of the responsible ownership, management, financial interest or personal business activities,
- Disregard of legal formalities and the failure to maintain arm's length relationships among related entities,
- The use of the corporate entity to procure labor, services or merchandise for another person or entity,
- Diversion of assets to a stockholder to detriment of creditors, or manipulation of assets and liabilities between entities to put the assets in one and the liabilities in another,
- Contracting with intent to avoid performance by a corporate entity to shield against liability, or as subterfuge of illegal transactions, and

- Formation and use of a corporation to transfer to it the existing liability of another person or entity.

Doing any of these things is a bad idea and if you or your business is sued in the future you risk the legal protections to you as an individual being lost.

How does this play out in the real world? There are many circumstances that may cause a person to sue you and your corporation. Here are some of them...

You're accused of fraud, lying or misrepresentation which caused some kind of harm to the plaintiff and your corporation is seen as the tool used to accomplish this.

Judges and jury members are human beings. We all have a sense that if someone was unjustly harmed, they should be made whole and the evil doer responsible should be punished. Of all of the factors that courts look at, the existence of fraud, wrongdoing or injustice is a flashing red light when deciding if corporate veil is a scam or not. In most cases the plaintiff is trying to go after shareholders or another, related company because of the alleged wrongdoing of the company or its owners.

It can happen something like,

- A creditor of Cosmo Corp successfully sues it and receives a final judgment for money damages,

- Cosmo Corp doesn't want to pay the judgment so it shuts down,

- It transfers all of its assets to Shazaam Corp. and it operates a substantially similar business with the same shareholders, management, assets and same employees as Cosmo.

If this is the case it's likely that Cosmo Corporation engaged in wrongful, potentially fraudulent actions, by shutting down its business and essentially reopening a new corporation. This is a classic example of a debtor attempting to defraud its creditor.

Before taking any steps that may be questionable, think about the situation from an outsider's perspective. If your action may appear to be fraudulent or just questionable, you should consult legal counsel to talk about the situation and your options. You may be able to accomplish what you want though steps may be more complicated than you thought but the end result may be an "arm's length" transaction that can withstand court scrutiny.

Failure to maintain the separate identities of the companies.

In an effort to try to protect yourself you form several related affiliates or multiple companies under the umbrella of one company but you fail to create and maintain separate identities of the companies.

You set up a parent company that operates and controls a subsidiary, the company provides the financing, they have the same officers, address, corporate information and your company files consolidated taxes with the subsidiary. If this is the case the subsidiary would likely be accused of being the alter ego of the parent company.

Failure to maintain separate identities of the company and its owners or shareholders.

Instead of companies being mingled together the issue whether a corporation or LLC is intertwined with the owners or shareholders of the companies. This can happen if an individual creates a corporation or LLC for his or her current business but continues to function as a sole proprietor. He or she uses individual checking accounts, ignores corporate formalities and uses company's assets as if they were his or her own.

There needs to be a barrier between the company and the owners. Owners, shareholders and officers must avoid commingling funds and treat assets of the business separate from personal assets.

Failure to adequately capitalize the company.

Though this alone wouldn't be enough for a court to find one company is the alter ego for another or for an individual, it can be used as evidence to support such a claim. Judges normally don't punish a company for poor management or a failure to be profitable but courts will take a look at the assets of the company to decide if the company's level of assets available to creditors is fair.

When a corporation opens it should have its own bank account with an adequate amount of money and/or assets to account for business operations. Owners should not open a business "on paper" and use their personal bank accounts, hoping to turn a profit then invest money back into the business. This conduct can jeopardize legal protections that normally come with incorporating or creating an LLC.

Failure to follow corporate formalities

You may not like formalities. Maybe you thought you could escape them by starting your own business and do things your own way. That's true to a point, but when it comes to creating a business entity you need to pay attention to the details or if you end up getting sued the time and money spent to create that corporation will have been wasted.

Though every corporate formality may not need to be met precisely, generally, if formalities aren't properly followed a court may decide the legal liability protection that shareholders planned on having was waived and their personal assets could be reached by a plaintiff. This often happens in smaller, family owned businesses, which may be less concerned with maintaining corporate records or may simply be too overwhelmed running their business to keep up with this task.

Based on the type of business created, whether it's a corporation or LLC, the owners or officers need to know the required legal formalities. This includes,

- Properly updating by-laws,
- Maintaining stock or membership ledgers,
- Holding initial and annual meetings of directors, managers and officers,
- Maintaining their status by filing an annual report,
- Business activities should be documented and records should be adequately kept and stored, and
- Those doing business with the company should be made aware of the corporate status of the company.

Creating a legal entity is a good start. But if you take the wrong actions and/or fail to take the necessary actions in order to maintain the protections that come with holding shares in an S corporation or being a member of an LLC, creating that entity "on paper" will be a waste of your time, effort and money.

Get Sufficient Business Insurance

Depending on the issue the liability you and your business faces could be addressed by coverage of an insurance policy. It could afford you a legal defense and potentially pay for a settlement or judgment against you.

Commercial insurance may be one of the most important ongoing financial investments you make in your company. You may not like paying the premiums but if something unexpected comes up it may be the difference between keeping your business going or filing for bankruptcy.

Commercial insurance may protect your business from common threats like property damage, business interruption, theft, liability due to negligence or employment practices and worker injury.

This coverage can be purchased from an insurance broker-agent. Before signing any checks verify the person's insurance license with the California Department of Insurance. Though insurance fraud is best known for people and businesses filing false or inflated claims, it also includes scam artists posing as insurance agents collecting premiums and disappearing.

Depending on the risks involved in your business, the broker-agent should present you with different coverage options. Ultimately, it's your responsibility to make an informed decision and choose the insurance that best fits your business.

You can choose from a wide range of coverages to protect you and your business, but they basically fall into two categories, property and casualty insurance.

Property insurance covers property that's stolen, damaged or destroyed by a covered peril. It includes commercial property, inland marine (loss or damage of items in transit), boiler and machinery and crime. Some of the more law-related property coverage you should take a look at include,

- Legal liability and product liability: This covers your legal liability for loss or damage to real and personal property of others as the result of negligent acts and/or omissions. The loss or damage must be caused by a peril covered by your policy.

- Building ordinance or law: This covers a situation where the enforcement of any building, zoning or land use law results in a loss to the undamaged portion of your building, the demolition and removal costs of undamaged parts of the structure or any increased cost of repairs or reconstruction.

- Crime insurance: This provides protection for the assets of your business including merchandise for sale, real property, money and securities. It may cover losses due to robbery, burglary, larceny, forgery and embezzlement.

Casualty insurance provides coverage for potential liability exposure of a person, business or organization. This potential liability can come from the negligent acts and omissions of an individual, business or organization that causes bodily injury and/or property damage to a third party. Some of the most common casualty insurance includes,

- Commercial automobile: This is similar to coverage you carry on your personal vehicle but commercial automobile exposures are more complex, depending on the needs of your business. Commercial automobile coverage protects your company from liability due to vehicles used in your business or any damage to the covered vehicles.

- Commercial general liability (CGL): This is comprehensive coverage covering all the hazards within the scope of the insurance policy that are not otherwise excluded. There are three sections making up a CGL policy: premises liability, products liability and completed operations. Premises liability covers liability for accidental injury or property damage due to a condition on your premises or operations. Products liability coverage is for any business that manufactures, sells, handles or distributes goods or products. It covers the potential liability for bodily injury or property damage caused by your goods or products. Completed operations: This is for your potential liability for bodily injury or property damage caused by your completed work.

If a liability claim is greater than the aggregate limit of liability, the policy limits are exhausted. If you buy commercial umbrella coverage you can protect your business from being liable for this excess liability judgment. Commercial umbrella coverage handles the amount of loss above the limits of a basic liability policy. Commercial automobile, CGL, workers compensation, or any liability policy can be covered by a commercial umbrella.

One option you could consider is a business owners policy (BOP). Designed for small businesses it's a combination commercial policy covering property, general liability and business interruption. It may be a good fit for small businesses such as hardware stores, barbershops, greeting card shops, accountant offices or low-density apartment houses.

Directors and officers (D&O) insurance is a form of management liability insurance which is designed to provide coverage to directors and officers of an entity, as well as the entity itself, against claims and lawsuits for wrongful acts committed in their capacity as directors or officers of the entity.

D&O liability coverage is key to any business. Insurance companies normally provide the following coverages in California,

- Losses that directors and officers could become personally liable for and for which they don't receive indemnification (a promise to cover their exposure) from the entity.
- Losses that entities pay to or on behalf of directors and officers as indemnification.
- Losses that the entity becomes liable to pay in connection with securities claims.
- Investigative expenses in connection with shareholder derivative demands.

Another type of liability coverage you should consider is Employment Practices Liability Insurance (EPLI) especially as the number of employees grows. In standard CGL policies they exclude legal claims against management based on employment law, including,

- Discrimination: Failure to hire or any other wrongful treatment of employees or job applicants based on their race, sex, religion, sexual orientation, age, disability or other status that is protected by federal, state or local law.

- Harassment: Unwelcome conduct by a supervisor, fellow employee, contractor or customer of either a sexual or non-sexual nature that creates a hostile work environment.

- Wrongful termination: Any actual or alleged wrongful dismissal, discharge or termination of employment, including breach of contract.

When making employment related decisions you may have acted in good faith and in compliance with applicable laws, but a current or former employee may not see it that way and sue you for actions you took relating to his or her employment.

Workers compensation coverage is mandated by state law. It covers your liability if an employee suffers a work related injury or illness. It provides benefits based on the type of illness or injury sustained.

Partner with a Business Attorney to Prevent Legal Problems for Your Business and Help You Address Them When They Happen

This book has some, but not nearly all, the legal issues a business owner may face. Spend enough time and money (and go to law school) and you too can gain expertise in these issues. Or, you can partner with a business attorney who can help you avoid problems that can threaten your business. If such problems arise that attorney could help you minimize the damage or defuse the situation.

There are many legal issues you could face.

- Will that employee angry at being fired sue you? Will he start working for a competitor?

- That major customer is disputing a valid and very large bill. What should you do if it's not paid?

- You want to lease a new, larger space to expand your business but the lease you've been given to sign is pages and pages long with print you need to squint to see.

If you could hire your own, part-time, in-house counsel, you would have expertise that's just a phone call or email away. Instead of guessing what to do, going with your gut or spending hours of research trying to determine the best path forward, an attorney could be there to protect your business.

With the help of your legal partner you may find yourself thinking and being more proactive. Instead of getting an employee handbook off the internet, you could use one that actually meets your particular needs. If a supplier or contractor hands you a contract to sign you can have it reviewed by someone familiar with contract law who could warn you about certain language, suggest changes or give you a draft contract you could hand back to that supplier or contractor.

If out of the blue you get a letter or phone call from an attorney or other party threatening legal action against you, you need not push the panic button. Hand it off to your legal partner to deal with and if there's a genuine issue, you can work together to come up with the best resolution.

It's a complicated world for small businesses, but with a lawyer to work with you, you'll be in a better position to cope with the many legal challenges that may threaten your business.

Business owners need to protect themselves from potential, personal liability in order to keep their businesses going in case they're accused of a wrongful act or negligence. That can take the forms of creating a business entity, purchasing insurance and working with an attorney.

If a business owner knows he or she has some protections against legal liability there can be some peace of mind and can be better able to focus on running and growing their business.

Mistake No. 2

Not Getting It in Writing

Written Contracts Provide Clarity and Protection

"If the deal is worth your time, put it in writing. It does not take that much time to get it in writing." - Tony T. Liu

---

The second legal mistake I see is business owners don't get their agreements in writing. Entrepreneurs tend act. They go out, talk to people, make deals, they hustle to turn their plans into reality. They may want to show their clients they're men and women of action, they're efficient and care about their clients, so they fulfill their parts of the agreement before they identify and write down the details of an agreement.

There needs to be a measure of trust when you work with clients, customers, suppliers, contractors and other businesses you partner with to succeed. But that trust has to be balanced by common sense. Since imperfect people are at the heart of the business community, you can't assume no one (including yourself) will never make a mistake, won't forget something or won't try to take advantage of you.

If there's a relationship that's important to your business it's a good idea to at least consider formalizing that relationship in writing. It's a way that both parties can protect themselves. Being asked, or asking another, to have duties and responsibilities of a relationship put into writing shouldn't be seen as an insult or a sign of distrust. It's a sign that a party is smart and wants to protect the relationship because it may prevent problems from worsening to the point the relationship breaks down.

Formalizing an important relationship into a written contract, though it may take some time and energy, is one of the most critical things a business owner can do to prevent legal problems. If they do arise, a written contract can help limit those problems and make them easier and quicker to resolve.

Contract Law Basics

A contract is a legally enforceable agreement between two or more parties that creates a binding obligation to do or not do particular things. A "party" can be a person, company or other legal entity. A contract must involve,

- Parties who are mentally competent to enter into a contract and authorized to do so.
- A mutual agreement by the parties. There is a "meeting of the minds" on the matter.
- An exchange of "consideration" (a legal term for something of value) between the parties. This can include a party not doing something it's able to do or has a right to do. Without consideration a supposed contract might be seen as an unenforceable promise.

If one party doesn't live up to its obligations it would "breach" the contract. If the other party can show the existence of a valid contract, the other party breached it and establish it suffered financial harm (damages) as a result, the party might sue to be reimbursed for those damages and/or a court order mandating the other party comply with the contract.

The statute of limitations, or deadline, to file a lawsuit concerning a contract starts at the time of the contract's breach and is two years for an oral contract and four years for a written one.

Why You Want a Contract in Writing

Not getting an agreement in writing is a big mistake. If the transaction is worth your time, get it in writing. It doesn't take much additional time to at least write down the details. If the contract is written it's easier to show the contract is valid and the parties' obligations to each other.

"Memory is generally not a problem, recall is." - *Tony T. Liu*

Memories fade, unfortunately. We are only humans. Some people may say they have a perfect memory. They just struggle with recall. For example, if you ask me what I had for breakfast today, I can tell you. I didn't have breakfast today. I woke up, got out my bag and came to work. I had coffee and one can of Monster energy drink. I did not put any solid food in my stomach.

If you ask me what I had for breakfast a month ago, I could not tell you off the top of my head. If I really need to know, I would look at my calendar and see what I did that day, who I met that morning, or where I was around 7:00 or 8:00 a.m. Hopefully, this would trigger my memory as to what I had for breakfast.

In addition, we do not, normally, recall agreements we make. What you think or believe you agreed to today may be different than your actual agreement with your partners, vendors or employees a year ago.

"A written agreement serves as a permanent historical document of a business transaction." - Tony T. Liu

---

Another benefit of a written agreement is that if you have a disagreement about what was agreed on, you can use it as a reference. You can pull it out and say, "Hey, one year ago, this is what we agreed on. These are the terms we discussed." You can flip to the back and say, "This is your signature, this is my signature, and the agreement was made on this date." That instrument is a permanent, historical document about the agreement between you, your vendors, your employees or your customers.

Putting something in writing also forces the parties to think about the situation, what they want to commit to and the possible consequences if they don't live up to the agreement.

With a written agreement you can evaluate it to identify whether changes need to be made before you sign it. You and the other party in the agreement can create a new agreement if you want to change the terms. Of course, if you decide to change the terms, you get them in writing and attach the new terms as an addendum to the original written agreement. Always get it in writing.

Without a written agreement your dispute becomes a he-said-she-said situation. You state your understanding of the agreement and the other person states their understanding. In the event of a big gap between what you believe and what the other party believes are the terms of the agreement, if you can't work something out you might end up in court to enforce your contractual rights or to defend yourself if the other party files a lawsuit against you.

This will require that you find witnesses who remember your version of the agreement and can testify on your behalf, or emails that show your version of the agreement between you and the other party is correct. With a written agreement, defending your version of the agreement is very easy. You simply attach that the written agreement to the court documents.

If you can do this the only dispute you may have is the other side didn't fulfill their contractual obligations. If so,

- You need to identify the reasons the other party has not fulfilled their obligations.

- The other party may have issues interpreting certain provisions in the contract, such as the price, quality, payment terms, etc., but they are easy to clarify and easy for a judge or fact finder to interpret because you can use your written agreement, not the testimony of witnesses stating who agreed to what.

If one party of the agreement is an intentional party, contract disputes are more burdensome because you must to go to court. Therefore, always get your agreements in writing.

A Contract Need Not Be in Writing to be Binding

You may want your important contracts in writing but you may be committing yourself to other types of contracts without being aware of it. In California a contract that's oral or one that's implied (created through a course of action between parties) could also be binding, they're just more difficult to prove and enforce. Through your words or actions you may be binding you or your business to a contract and potentially be sued by a party trying to enforce it.

- Oral: Since there's nothing written down, the party being sued could deny (rightly or wrongly) there was such a contract or the terms were not as the plaintiff claims.

- Implied: This contract (or quasi contract) is based on the conduct of the parties. A party who knowingly accepts a benefit from another under circumstances where the benefit is not a "gift" under the law (if it was a gift, there's no need for any action in response). Under the circumstances, the party accepting the benefit is under a legal obligation to give fair value for the benefit received. This is the most difficult type of contract to enforce.

In your dealings with other parties you should be aware that what you say and do might be interpreted as creating a contract. As best you can avoid these types of situations and if you think one might arise make it clear to the other party you're not committing to any agreement.

Contracts Terms You Should Be Aware of

Whether you want the other party to agree to a contract or a draft has been sent to you, there are important elements of a contract that should be included. You should get an attorney involved in the drafting or approval of any contract to make sure it's written in a way that serves or protects your interests. Here are parts of contracts that are normally included,

- Definitions: These should spell out and clarify the important terms in the contract. If there is a conflict involving a contract it literally could turn on the meaning of one or a few words. A definition could be the item or service you're agreeing to purchase along with specifications or a description. You need to read all the definitions in a proposed contract and get changes or clarifications for any definition you don't understand or agree with.

- Obligations: The contract should clearly state all that the parties are expected to do and under what circumstances. If there are more obligations for you and/or fewer obligations for the other party than you originally intended, there needs to be a discussion between the parties, clarification of the obligations and changes made as necessary.

- Costs: How much will be paid for the product or service? If other aspects are changed (quantity, quality, deadlines) have the parties agreed to a change in price? If so, what? Is there a mechanism allowing prices to go up over a period of time?

- Conditions: Do certain actions or events need to happen before one or both parties needs to do something in response? If so, are these conditions realistic? If a condition isn't met, is there a "Plan B" or some way in which a party needs to change its actions?

- Authority: Does the person signing the contract have the authority to legally bind the other party? Does the other party have implied or apparent authority to sign the contract? Does he or she need explicit, higher authority to act by a company officer or board of directors? If you act unreasonably and the contract is signed by someone clearly acting beyond his or her authority, the other party may not obligated to comply with the contract.

- Term: Does the contract explicitly state a date when the contract automatically ends? Is it meant to go on indefinitely, as long as the parties are happy with the agreement?

- Amendments: The contract should state under what circumstances a future change in the contract can be negotiated.

- Complete: Are all the relevant terms and issues in the contract? Does the contract incorporate language or terms on a document other than the contract? If so, do you know what it is and understand it? Don't assume the parties agree to or understand something that's not in the contract. It may have a clause stating the parties' complete obligations and understandings are contained in the document. If something needs to be added, that needs to be done before the contract is signed.

- Remedies: Are there penalties if one side or the other does not perform and the contract is breached? What happens if deadlines aren't met? The quality is insufficient? What damages, if any, does the breaching party agree to pay? Does this include costs and attorney's fees of the party harmed by the breach?

- Default: What happens if the business receiving the goods or service defaults on payment? How is that defined? Do payments need to be made within a certain time frame? Is there a penalty if a payment is late or partial? Can the other party quickly and easily end the contract in case of a default?

- Dispute resolution: There should be language in the contract stating ways the parties can resolve any disputes concerning the performance of the contract. It may mandate the parties not sue in court, but instead have the issue resolved in a mediation or an arbitration. There may be language stating that the laws of a certain state be used when deciding the outcome of a dispute.

- Termination: Under what circumstances can a party terminate the contract? How much notice needs to be given to the other party? Are there any penalties to terminating the contract?

Potential Defenses to Enforcing a Contract

Contract law cuts both ways. You may want to enforce a contract against the other party or the other party may want to enforce it against you.

Perhaps you entered into a contract in the past which you simply can no longer comply with or the situation has changed and you're losing too much money living up to the contract. As much as you are a person of your word, economically it may not make sense to comply with the contract.

Defenses are helpful to know when drafting a contract in order to try to prevent their use in the future. They can also help void a contract whose terms are impossible or too difficult to follow. Here are some defenses to the enforcement of a contract,

- Ambiguity: The terms are too vague to be fully complied with.
- Failure to mitigate damages: The party trying to enforce the contract didn't take reasonable steps to lessen the harm done by the contract's breach. The party breaching the contract shouldn't have to pay for the other party's laziness or inattentiveness.

- Changed terms: The enforcing party is trying to change the terms of the contract without the other party's consent. The alleged contract the other party is trying to enforce doesn't exist because there was no mutual agreement.

- There is no breach of contract: The party did what was required and if it didn't, that failure is excused under the facts of the case and applicable law.

- Tender of payment: The party offered full payment but the other party refused to accept it.

- Substantial compliance: The party complied with most of the contract's obligations, except for others that are unimportant or didn't cause any harm.

- Failure to disclose: The other party failed to disclose important information making compliance with the contract impossible.

- Unclean hands/unjust enrichment: The other party committed wrongdoing and is trying to profit from it. It would be unfair if the party receives the money it seeks.

- Invalid/illegal contract: The contract is not valid, it's illegal and can't be enforced because of fraud, deceit and/or misrepresentation.

- Lack of acceptance: The party didn't agree to the contract or certain terms of the contract.

- Lack of consideration: The party didn't receive any goods or services, received them late or they were defective or services were substandard.

- Duress/undue influence: You were forced to enter into the contract because the other party took unfair advantage of your mental state or by using threats or force.

- Impossibility or impracticability: The contract can't be complied because it's not possible or practical to do so.

- Failure of condition precedent: The other party didn't comply with a specific term or condition of the contract which it was required to do before the party had to pay.

- Statute of limitations: The other party failed to file its lawsuit in time, four years from the date of the breach.

There are a number of contracts you should consider creating in writing that can help protect you and your business.

Agreements with Fellow Shareholders or LLC Members

If it's more than you as the shareholder or member of your corporation or LLC you should protect yourself and your business by creating written agreements with others involved in your business.

A shareholder agreement is a contract between shareholders spelling out how the corporation will be run and what happens if certain events occur. These agreements are important for corporations with a small number of shareholders who are active in the corporation's daily business operations.

A shareholder agreement written before a corporation is started (or a member agreement before an LLC is formed) is like a prenuptial agreement before a couple is married. It forces the parties to talk about their future and what happens if the relationship ends.

The parties should discuss what they're bringing to the business, the parties' expectations, what should happen if a shareholder wants to leave the business, how and for what price shares can be sold and how disputes can be resolved. It's a blue print for how the business will be run in the future. Any matters not covered in the shareholder agreement are governed by the state's corporate laws.

State law gives shareholders the right to vote for who will manage the corporation (the board of directors) but the law doesn't give shareholders the legal right to be a director or to hold any corporate office. Through a shareholder agreement the shareholders can get a contractual right to be a director and/or officer of the corporation.

Buy Sell Agreements

A shareholder agreement normally includes provisions regarding stock ownership and sales. An important provision is when the corporation and a shareholder can sell his or her stock to a third party or how one shareholder can sell shares to another.

The corporation in the future may want to exchange shares for an investment in the company. If a shareholder wants to leave the business there should be a mechanism by which current shareholders are able to buy them or allow an outside party to purchase them. Since these small businesses aren't publicly traded, there needs to be a formula or process to set the price if there's a sale. Shareholders may also want to spell out what happens if one of them gets divorced (potentially resulting in partial ownership by the other spouse) or declares personal bankruptcy.

Every shareholder and membership agreement should have a section devoted to succession planning. Though we may fantasize about the long, rewarding and remarkably illness-free retirement that awaits us in warm and friendly surroundings, we don't like thinking about what may happen if we suddenly become seriously ill, injured or unexpectedly die. Because of the realities we face, shareholders and members need to think about what should happen in case a shareholder (especially a majority shareholder) or member can no longer manage the business.

Ideally planning for succession should be done years in advance of a retirement or unexpected departure of an owner. There should be a management structure created that won't rely too heavily on the business owner to survive. Whether the business is being transferred to family, employees, shareholders, members or a third party, the business will be less valuable if the owner is so essential to its operation it will shut down without him or her.

Failing to plan for succession could be a disaster for the long term future of a business since many closely held businesses fail shortly after the founder leaves the scene. One of the benefits of a corporation or LLC is that it can survive the founder, put not if sufficient planning doesn't take place.

When creating this plan, the business owners should consider,

- Their needs and those of their families,
- Whether a capable successor is available to manage the business,
- Whether that person's a family member or someone outside the family,
- Whether another shareholder, member or an outside party should purchase the person's share of the business,
- The future prospects of the business, and,

- When the shareholder or member is willing to transfer control of the business.

This can be done a number of ways and should match the particular circumstances of the business. A common part of succession planning is a "buy sell" agreement among the shareholders or members which serves many purposes. It can,

- Protect the business from disputes between shareholders or members concerning management rights, dividends and voting deadlocks.

- Allow a stockholder, member or the company to buy the shares of an owner or part owner who retires, becomes disabled or dies, or wants to sell shares to a third party.

- Provides a source of funds to the selling shareholder or his or her estate.

- Spell out what shareholders or members can do in case one of them gets divorced or declares bankruptcy.

Resolving Disputes

Whether you formed a corporation or LLC, a big step to manage expectations and make sure everyone knows their responsibilities is an effective shareholder or member agreement, LLC operating agreement or shareholders agreement.

A shareholder or member agreement should state how disputes will be resolved. It's virtually inevitable shareholders will have some disagreements along the way, the only questions are the reason for the disagreement and how serious it will be. To avoid expensive and time-consuming legal action parties can state how certain disputes will be resolved. This can include mediation (where a neutral third party tries to help the parties reach a resolution), arbitration (an alternate dispute resolution mechanism involving a private trial of sorts lead by an arbitrator or panel of arbitrators) or the appointment of a non-shareholder director to break voting deadlocks.

If despite agreement owners are at a stalemate or relationships have simply broken down it may be time for disputes to be resolved or for people to go their own ways. How this takes place should be spelled out in the agreement which should be tailored to the needs of the business and the owners. If there is no such agreement state statutes cover these topics in a "one size fits all" approach that may or may not work very well.

If things are going poorly you may want the other owners out, they may want you out or both. It's possible that the company's not doing well and everyone's miserable. Maybe it's going very well and some are trying to get more of their fair share of the profits.

If there is an agreement,

- Who has the ability to make what decisions for the business?
- Has one or more parties over-stepped their bounds?
- Have obligations been met?
- If the agreement has been breached, are remedies spelled out in it?
- How are disagreement supposed to be resolved?
- If the parties can't do it themselves, must a mediator or arbitrator be used?
- If the disagreement goes to court, must it be filed in a particular place using the laws of a specified state?
- Does the agreement state attorney's fees and costs of litigation can be awarded to the prevailing party?
- Can a judge or arbitrator award attorney's fees?

If you've reached the point of no return and feel somebody needs to leave,

- Try to avoid litigation. It's expensive, time consuming, energy intensive, emotional and a distraction from running the business. If costs and attorney's fees can be awarded to the prevailing party, it ups the costs considerably. Trials are unpredictable and outcomes uncertain. How much risk are you willing to tolerate?

- If you do end up in litigation it may be for any number of reasons. You may be sued. You may need to get a restraining order to prevent another owner from using company assets for personal gain or to start another business.

- Even though avoiding lawsuits has many benefits, if there will be lawsuits there are benefits to being the plaintiff and not waiting to be sued. If you file first, you can try to set the narrative of the conflict which is that you are the good guy. You also have the first choice as to where the lawsuit will be filed.

Considerations for Family Owned Businesses

America is filled with family run businesses, large and small. Working with family members has many potential benefits and costs. If things are going well and there are no major conflicts or disagreements, both the business and the family can benefit. If disagreements are serious and can't be amicably resolved both family relationships can suffer as can the business, which may lose critical people with important skills, contacts or experience. That person may also start working for or start his or her own competing business.

Every family owned business should also have a shareholder or membership agreement that also spells out how conflicts should be resolved (including a buy sell agreement), who owns what share of the business, who has the power to do what and how the business will be managed.

When a family owned business makes the jump from a sole proprietorship or partnership to become a corporation or LLC, it's an excellent time to step back and think about ways the business can be structured and ways of dispute resolution can be incorporated into a business through an agreement by the parties.

Those structures should consider,

- Preparation for complications: If family and business relationships will intertwine you need to be prepared by carefully thinking about each party's interests and how they might collide.

- Striving for transparency: Prior to talking about business matters, start a conversation about the challenges and issues the business faces. Come up with means and methods to resolve conflicts when they arise. Creating rules and setting expectations before conflicts happen can make resolution easier.

- Consulting a neutral party: If there's a particularly contentious issue or issues, you may want to hire a neutral third party such as a mediator, family therapist or trusted friend. An outside, neutral perspective may help you get to the heart of the problems and reach a resolution.

Contracts with Employees

Employment contracts are becoming more common, especially as employers become more concerned with protecting their intellectual property and seek to channel any employment related disputes away from the courts and towards arbitration.

How far your business wants to take this is up to you. You could have all or none or your employees sign contracts or you may just target management or those whose departure may be particularly damaging if they decide to work for a competitor or start their own competing business.

On the plus side,

- In your contract you could include a sign-on bonus in exchange for a legally binding promise by the employee not to reveal confidential information he or she learns while working for you.

- You can spell out the rights and obligations of both parties at the start of the employment relationship. An employee may want spelled out the basis for any bonuses or how time off is earned while you could state that travel is required as part of the job.

- One thing to clarify is that the employment relationship is "at will" and either party can end the relationship at any time, with or without notice and for any lawful reason. A contract could spell out the fact the job is for a specific period or both sides need to give a notice of termination.

- Both sides can feel more secure because expectations are spelled out. A manager may feel more secure which may improve his or her morale, productivity and loyalty to your company. The company may feel more secure in investing in training and feel that turnover is less likely.

- Your company can better protect its interests. You could include provisions that forbid release of trade secrets. If the person is inventing or designing a product a trade secrets provision can ensure the end results are "works for hire" and his or her rights are automatically assigned to your company. A binding arbitration clause would require the parties to address any work related legal disputes through arbitration.

On the down side,

- A contract may provide an employee additional remedies if the relationship ends badly. Without a contract if an ex-employee sues you he or she would need to rely on statutory or common law (law developed by the courts over the years) for relief. If there's a contract, a breach of contract claim could be added to the list of causes of action.

- Terminating the person's job may be more difficult. Without a contract the relationship is "at will" and either party can end it at any time, with or without notice and with or without cause. Depending on the language of the contract a court may only allow a termination if there is "good cause" to fire the person.

- There are some administrative burdens and costs. Drafting these documents can consume resources and keeping track of contracts with notice requirements or different renewal dates could be cumbersome.

- If there's a dispute between you and the employee it may require a judge or arbitrator to interpret the contract. There are pros and cons to drafting more broad and more specific contracts. A contract may have language that's broad in one section but specific in others. A very vague contract may not help you much but a very specific, complex, lengthy one will be more resource consuming to create and may make it less likely that the employee will sign it. Ultimately, no matter how it's worded, a judge or arbitrator may be the one determining the parties' rights and responsibilities, not you.

Contracts with Independent Contractors

If you rely heavily on a contractor you should have a contract to protect you. This contractor could provide an important service that keeps your business going, like IT services, or it can be a freelancer who does important work for you. These contractors allow you to get extra help, fulfill a specific need and give you flexibility while you avoid the costs of hiring additional people or buying additional equipment.

It may be a good idea to formalize the relationship with a written contract. You can spell out what each party expects from each other, what will be done or delivered when, a mechanism to work out disputes (if all else fails, you may want to mandate mediation and/or arbitration, not litigation, to reach a resolution), prices, when payment will be made and if a party wants to break off the relationship a time frame for notice should be given.

You should make it clear the parties intend the person is an independent contractor, not an employee and he or she is responsible for paying his or her own taxes and is responsible for his or her own workers compensation coverage. Though this language isn't necessarily binding if the person later claims to be your employee, it may be helpful in case of a legal dispute.

Contracts with Suppliers

If your business manufactures or assembles your end product, you're an importer, sell something made by another business or your business is a restaurant, you are dependent on suppliers for your business' survival. If your supply is delayed, stopped or what you're receiving isn't of high enough quality you could be in big trouble.

A supplier contract is one between your business and a supplier. It's important because it documents the terms of your agreement that in exchange for your payments you will receive certain goods or products, perhaps at specific times, of a certain quality at a given price.

There can be a given way by which the parties will communicate with each other changes in what's needed and how and when the supply may change. There could be mechanisms by which price increases can be worked out and a notice period if one party wants to re-negotiate or end the contract.

A way to work out disagreements should be included. If they can't be resolved a clause could mandate the parties bring the issue to a mediator and/or arbitration and avoid lawsuits against each other.

If you have this contract in place and your supplier breaches it by suddenly increasing prices or ends your supply without notice, this agreement can help you cover the harm done by increased prices or the fact you need to scramble to find another supplier or your sales have dropped due to the lack of inventory. With the help of your written contract you can put your supplier on notice of your legal rights and work out a resolution, or, failing that, if your losses are serious enough, file a lawsuit or take the matter to arbitration or file a lawsuit.

Contract With a Joint Partner

Like marriages, joint ventures don't always work out. The joint venture may have been a bad idea to begin with, the market may not have been as strong or as mature as the companies hoped or perhaps the parties just didn't work well together. A piece by Patricia Farrell in Entrepreneur magazine well stated the "seven deadly sins" that frequently break up joint ventures.

- Gluttony: Many joint ventures use up their initial capital much faster than expected. Failure to properly plan for the possibility that resources may be consumed too quickly may result in unwise loan to raise funds. Prudent joint venture members will anticipate the need for additional capital and determine acceptable sources of funding in the initial joint venture agreement.

- Wrath: Arguments over control can occur because partners are used to having control. Compromise about how to run the joint venture may not be easy. The relationship may fall apart and partners may no longer want to work together. Partners should assume that there will be conflicts at some point. If a board of directors with representatives from both companies is appointed to make decisions about how to run the venture, they can then hire employees or contractors to manage the day-to-day operations. The joint venture agreement should spell out the decisions to be made by management and which ones need board approval.

- Lust: Desire for a partner's assets can result in serious mistakes that may undermine the venture and the relationship with the partner. Venture partners should make sure that each partner's assets (such as intellectual property, capital or equipment) are appropriately valued and translated into reasonable shares of ownership and control.

- Pride: Most entrepreneurs take great pride in their company's culture but when two company cultures combine, pride can lead to unproductive arguments about using one company's methods over another. Partners should discuss in advance how to handle cultural differences and train managers to help employees adapt to differences in company cultures.

- Greed: Partners want to see profits from the venture as quickly as possible, but distributing profits isn't always as simple as giving each party a share proportionate to their ownership. There may be priorities for distributions, such as loan repayment or reinvesting a portion of the profits. The joint venture agreement should lay out how and when profits will be distributed and the order of priority in which they will be distributed.

- Envy: Many joint ventures are created by two companies that operate in the same or similar industries to accomplish a specific project. Their competitive interests can create mistrust and envy between partners that may ultimately cause the venture to fail. The joint venture agreement should set specific boundaries regarding information that must be freely shared and information that can be restricted. The agreement could also determine how one or both companies will restructure to avoid any conflict of interest.

- Sloth: Founding partners may be slow to plan their exit strategy, assuming it can wait until the venture is up and running. Partners should from the beginning of the joint venture, consider all possible scenarios in which the joint venture may end. They should lay out the terms and conditions for a variety of end scenarios to avoid arguments down the road.

Because there are so many ways a joint venture can go wrong there needs to be a written contract between the parties addressing these deadly sins and other potential problems. It should spell out how conflicts between the parties can be resolved and if they can't, how will the entity be wound up? Can one party buy out the other, and if so, at what price? Could the entity be split apart with different pieces going to each party? If an amicable parting of the ways can't be worked out, is mediation or arbitration required or can a party just file a lawsuit?

Digital Contracts

Can you be bound by a contract that only exists in a digital document that's signed electronically? Under California law, under specific circumstances, such a contract can be valid and enforceable.

California's Uniform Electronic Transactions Act (UETA) aided the ability to use electronic means to conduct business. If the parties to the contract follow the law and its 17 subsections, they can form binding contracts or conduct business electronically, without exchanging signatures on paper.

The UETA requires that the parties need to agree to conduct the transaction electronically. This agreement can be shown from the context and surrounding circumstances of the situation, including the parties' conduct.

The definition of "electronic signature" includes an electronic sound, symbol, or process attached to or logically associated with an electronic record and executed or adopted by a person with the intent to sign the electronic record.

The law states that no record, signature, or contract can be denied legal effect or enforceability only because it's in electronic form or an electronic record was used in its creation. If a law mandates that information be provided in writing but the parties have agreed to conduct a transaction through electronic means, the written requirement is satisfied by providing an electronic record "capable of retention by the recipient" when it was received.

The law also states that an electronic signature is attributable to a person if it was the act of the person and that can be shown in any manner, including by showing of the efficacy of a security procedure used to determine it was actually the person who agreed to it.

If you want your business to use these types of contracts you need to use procedures complying with UETA's many requirements. There needs to be evidence both parties agreed to conduct the transaction by electronic means and there needs to be evidence the electronic signature is the act of the person who allegedly signed.

Contract Mistakes Companies Commonly Make

There are many contract mistakes that business owners and managers can make. Depending on the circumstances a mistake could be not a big deal or a major problem. Here are some of them.

The Contract Wasn't Written by or Reviewed the Company's Lawyer

You may think the services of an attorney are expensive, but what's the potential cost of not getting an attorney's help? A contract given you may appear simple enough, but that simplicity may be due to the fact it's vague (when in this case a more precise and technical contract would be in your interests) or a boilerplate form bought online. An attorney can tell you the risks of signing it as is and suggest changes to help protect your business.

Not Investigating and Understanding Potential Business Partners

How well do you really know the party you'll be contracting with? You may have done the math on an expected return on investment, but what have you done to research the party with whom you'll be entering a legally binding contract? Has the owner of the other business been arrested or convicted of fraud? Has the business been sued or sued others involved in prior contracts or other disputes? You should also do a credit search to learn about financial viability of your potential partner.

Due Diligence That's Insufficient or Non-Existent

If the other party isn't a frequent filer in court, doesn't have a criminal record and appears to have sufficient funds, more research awaits because due diligence should be performed. What you can do may be limited by your time and resources and the contract's value may not be great enough to justify a big investment in time and energy, but making sure this is the right deal, the right arrangement or partnership for you can help you avoid huge headaches in the future. Contract language should also include a provision stating compensation would be owed if representations, warranties or other contractual assumptions later prove to be false or inaccurate.

Not Defining Important Terms and Including Ambiguous Language

So the parties can fulfill their intent, contracts need to have well defined terms and unambiguous provisions. A party seeking to void a contract, or just a section, may claim the key language is ambiguous and could be interpreted a number of ways. Careful drafting can close possible loopholes.

Not Having a Choice of Law Provision

Does your contract involve a party from a different state? Will its performance cross state lines? If the agreement falls apart and lawsuits are filed, under which jurisdiction and using which state's laws would be most advantageous to your business? The contract can spell out where such a lawsuit can be filed or which state law is to be used to interpret the contract. Contract law is state specific. California law may be very helpful or harmful depending on the situation.

Not Including Provisions Concerning Defaults, Opportunities to Cure and Termination

Though these topics raise the possibility of things not going well, they need to be addressed so your interests can be protected. They also encourage contract performance and may help avoid litigation. If a party is put on notice of a potential breach and an opportunity to solve the problem are required, parties are forced to try to work out their differences. They help the contract's chances of survival because breaches need to be addressed as they happen, instead of being allowed to fester (increasing potential financial harm) and become a source of conflict. Terms stating the duration of a contract and how and when it might be renewed or terminated are also very helpful. If a party is allowed to terminate the contract early harm done could be limited if unexpected, negative circumstances occur. Your business shouldn't be stuck in a bad relationship, costing you money, due to circumstances beyond your control.

Not Spelling Out Which Damages Would be Available in Case of a Breach or Dispute

Recovery could be limited to a given dollar amount or bar the recovery of specified damages. This language can help a party avoid unnecessary risks or liabilities and if the recovery is limited parties may be less likely to resort to expensive litigation in case of problems with the contract.

Not Having a Statement the Written Contract is the Final Expression of the Agreement

This should limit outside evidence that could be used to try to show the intent of the parties when they agreed to the contract. Normally this kind of provision states that the contract as written is the final expression of the parties' agreement and it supersedes prior communications and understandings and any changes need to be done through a written and signed amendment. This would make it harder to claim there are side agreements, other understandings or later modifications were made.

Not Stating How Disputes Will be Resolved

If the two sides can't resolve their differences, do they need to get the help of a mediator? Must they file for an arbitration or can they go to court?

Failing to Create Internal Procedures to Make Sure Both Parties are Complying With the Contract

Once the contract is signed, don't just throw it in a file. Don't just look at it if you think something is going wrong. Create procedures so performance by both parties can be monitored. You don't want to blunder your way into a legal dispute with your partner.

Contracts make the business world go round. If you educate yourself about contract issues and they're properly prepared you can lessen the chance an expensive, time and energy consuming legal battle over a contract will entangle you and your business.

Mistake No. 3
Employee Relations

Workers are critical to a business' success and future. A business owner can only do so much. If you want your business to be successful and grow you'll need to rely on others. The right workers doing the right work can make your business what you want it to be. The wrong people doing the wrong things can hold you back and potentially be a huge detriment to your plans.

Employment law issues are generally emotionally charged, so you must handle them professionally and delicately. A full account of all the legal issues you may have to deal with when it comes to workers could fill many volumes, not the chapter of a paperback book, so I will just hit some of the highlights.

Employment and labor law are highly technical areas of law. Making a mistake, even one made while you're doing your best and acting in good faith, could result in a lawsuit against your business.

If you have an issue with your employees or you perceive future issues may happen, consult with your attorney right away. Not only are employment laws complex they're ever changing. New laws may be passed, new regulations issued and courts continuously issue decisions interpreting these laws and regulations. Ensure you are following the current law because complying with an outdated one won't do you any good.

An example of the complexity of the law is what can happen if you hire someone but it doesn't take long for you to decide you hired the wrong person. He or she simply is not a good fit for what you need to get done. Generally speaking it's best to let the person go as quickly as possible because keeping them will affect your bottom line as well as your company culture and morale. However,

- If the person is, let's say, an Asian woman, while in the past you let an underperforming white male work for you for a year before he quit for another job. If you fire her you may be accused of sex or race discrimination.

- Shortly after the hiring you learn the employee filed a wage and hour or workers compensation claim against a prior employer. If you fire the employee soon after learning of this prior claim you could be accused of retaliation.

- While deciding whether or not to fire the person, you talk to his supervisor who mentions the new employee told him his wife has cancer. Since the new employee could be considered "associated" with someone with a disability, if you fire him you could be accused of disability discrimination.

While you may think that quickly firing a new hire who isn't a good fit should be a quick and easy thing to do, depending on the circumstances, it may also be quick and easy for a former employee to sue you.

Like any other area of law a plaintiff has the burden of proof and simply filing a lawsuit doesn't make allegations true. You may have any number of valid defenses but employers need to think of employee relations like a chess match. You shouldn't act on impulse, you need to think a couple steps ahead before making a decision that may end up with you being served with a lawsuit.

Is the Worker an Employee or Independent Contractor?

Employment laws generally cover employees, not independent contractors (with a few exceptions, depending on the jurisdiction). Hiring independent contractors to perform work has become increasingly common in our "gig" economy but it can be a legal minefield for the uninformed or unethical employer.

If there's a legal dispute whether a worker is an employee or independent contractor generally the key difference is how much control, potential or actually exercised, you have over the details of this person's work. What an employee does could have a critical impact on the overall well-being of a business. Because of that importance you may want to exercise a lot of control over the person, but if you do that, the person will more likely be classified as an employee, not an independent contractor, by a court or government agency.

Why is the distinction important? Employees normally come with a lot of expenses (taxes, benefits and increased regulation) and it may be cheaper to have an independent contractor. If you try to get that cheaper cost but actually have an employment relationship with the person, you open yourself up to legal claims for any number of things (such as wage and hour, missed health insurance, unpaid unemployment compensation insurance, failure to pay Social Security taxes, failure to provide workers compensation coverage...).

"Employees v. independent contractor status-it's all about the degree of control." - *Tony T. Liu*

If you want to outsource that work to an independent contractor then you need to give up close supervision of the person. You can detail what you want them to do and when the tasks been done, but the more control you want over the methods and means as to how something is done, the more likely the person is an employee under the law.

- Do you require that the person begin at 8:30 a.m. and leave at 5:00 p.m. with a 30-minute break every day?

- Do you require this person to complete a specific amount of work every day?

- Do you keep track of what is done?

- Must the person wear a uniform?
- Do you prohibit the person from working for a competitor?
- Do you supply tools or materials?
- Must the person use certain business cards or have a title which makes it appear to others he or she is an employee?
- Does the person need to attend meetings with your staff as if he or she is just another staff member?

If the answer is yes, then the person working for you is most likely an employee, not an independent contractor.

Your relationship with an independent contractor is more like your relationship with a vendor. An independent contractor is like a consultant who provides services for your company. If you are hiring a consultant would you ask this person to come work at 8:30 a.m., only have a 30 minute break and leave at 5:00 p.m. every day?

A few months ago, I was hired by a company in the process of negotiating a merchant acquisition. One company was trying to purchase another and one investor wanted me to be present at meetings and draft the contract on the spot. He paid my hourly fee, so I did not complain about the arrangement. I just cleared my calendar so I could attend the meetings.

I did whatever the company needed me to do. I was at the company from 10:00 a.m. to 6:00 p.m. for five days. Although I agreed with the arrangement, if I needed to leave, take a phone call from my office, or handle an emergency for my office, I did so during the down time ..

Yes, the company required me to be available for a certain period of time, especially on particular days during that week, so I could attend meetings, but I was a consultant the company paid for to take care of a specific need. Therefore, I did what they expected, but I did not restrict myself from taking care of my own law firm.

This illustrates the difference between an independent contractor and an employee. Yes, you can set expectations for your consultants or independent contractors, including specifying the end result, quality of the work, etc., and you can monitor your independent contractors on a daily or weekly basis, but if you have considerable control over these individuals' work hours, how they do their jobs, what they are required to do, etc., then they should be classified as employees.

"You may have an agreement with an independent contractor to perform certain tasks for your company, but if you treat this person like an employee, he/she is the employee." - Tony T. Liu

---

As you know I'm all about written contracts and if you hire an independent contractor you should have a written agreement with the person spelling out that the person is an independent contractor, not an employee. That said, such an agreement is just part of the puzzle when it comes to the worker's job classification. It's not *conclusive* evidence the person's an independent contractor, but it can be used as evidence to support your position the person's not an employee.

If the person later changes their mind and seeks unpaid wages or claims employment discrimination, your agreement may not be enforceable. A government agency or judge may give a lot more weight to the facts of the situation (especially the degree of potential and actual control you exercised) when deciding the person's status than the language of an agreement.

If you intentionally misclassify an employee as an independent contractor you are focusing on a short term solution instead of one that's long term. In the short run, you may be able to save money. In the long run, if this relationship dissolves, you could pay serious penalties.

- You may need to reimburse these employees for overtime, medical expenses that would've been covered by medical benefits, lunch breaks and vacation pay.

- If the person is injured on the job you could face severe penalties for not having workers compensation insurance covering him or her. Your company could be sued in a personal injury action, which could be far more expensive to defend and open up the possibility of much more expensive damages than what's available for a workers compensation claim.

One way to get yourself into trouble is in the hopes of saving money you fire employees then "hire" them back as independent contractors but treat them the same. It's just a matter of time before the complaints to government agencies or lawsuits are filed.

With the help of an attorney, identify the nature of your relationship with these individuals.If how something is done and close supervision are priorities, the person is probably an employee.

If you just need someone to provide you with a good or a service by a given deadline that meets certain requirements, but you don't care how or where that's accomplished, the person is more likely an independent contractor.

Once you figure that out, you can enter into a contract with the independent contractor or hire the person and hand over the employee handbook.

"If you need an employee, hire one. If you have a sufficient number of employees for your company, but you need additional help every so often, hire an independent contractor just for those circumstances. However, if you are trying to save hiring costs by contracting with independent contracts instead putting them on payroll, the negative consequences of misclassification generally outweigh any company savings." - Tony T. Liu

---

Is the Worker Exempt or an Hourly Employee?

Misclassification isn't just an issue when determining if the person is an employee or not. If you've decided the person you're hiring is an employee, on what basis will he or she be paid?

Employees can be classified into two categories: salaried or exempt employees and hourly wage earners.

- Salaried employees are generally professionals, managers, accountants, engineers, doctors, lawyers, etc., who get paid a specific amount on a weekly, biweekly or monthly basis.

- Wage earners get paid based on how many hours they work at your company, receive lunch breaks that you must provide and if your employees work more than eight hours a day, you must pay them overtime.

- To be considered exempt employees under California law employees generally customarily and regularly exercise discretion and independent judgment in their jobs. Discretion and independent judgment involve comparing and evaluating possible courses of action and making a decision after considering various possibilities.

- This classification can be very complicated and a person's duties may be a mix of what those in both categories do, so it's not difficult to get this wrong.

Employers my try to save money by avoiding paying overtime, so they classify their employees as salaried (though in some circumstances a salaried employee may be entitled to overtime pay). This may cause trouble if an employee is terminated and gets legal advice. The employee and his or her attorney may argue that although the employee was classified as a salaried employee, that employee was actually a wage earner. If so, an employee can claim unpaid overtime, break time, lunch hours, etc.

All businesses want to save money but cutting corners in this area of law is short-sighted. If you make a mistake or intentionally misclassify your employees, your costs will far outweigh whatever money you saved.

Misclassification is the most litigated matter in employment law cases. Always consult with your attorney regarding the right classification for specific positions within your company because employment law is very complicated and changes all the time.

Hiring Process Limitations

You can use whatever hiring process you choose as long as it doesn't break the law. You can't intentionally discriminate against those protected by anti-discrimination law (see below) through the hiring process or use a testing or screening process that has an illegal, adverse impact on a protected group.

You shouldn't inquire about a disability (other than asking if a reasonable accommodation would be needed to perform an essential function of the job) and you can have a physical exam after a conditional job offer, as long as that exam is used across the board to fill a position, not just used for an applicant that appears, or admits to being, disabled. That job offer can't be premised upon passing the exam.

Asking about whether a female candidate is or plans on becoming pregnant would also be a bad idea. Given marital status is a protected basis under California law even friendly chit chat about an applicant's family could come back to bite you if the person feels the person's marital status was used as a reason he or she didn't get the job.

Another prohibited inquiry includes requesting job applicants to disclose, or considering as a factor in hiring, information about an arrest or criminal detention that did not result in a conviction or a referral to, or participation in, a pretrial or post-trial diversion program.

Due to a recent change in state law an employer can't, orally or in writing, directly or indirectly, seek salary history information from an applicant. Salary history information is the person's rate of compensation and includes other benefits. This information can't be sought from the applicant's present or past employers either.

The law also mandates that employers, even if they have this information, can't rely on it as a reason to decide to hire, or not to hire, the applicant. If that person is hired past salary history can't be used as a factor in deciding what the new employee should be paid. The goal of the change in the law is to reduce the pay differential between men and women in the workplace.

Wage and Hour Issues

There are many potential issues when it comes to how to compensate your employees, including what breaks are needed when. Each situation is unique so if you have any questions, talk to an attorney.

Lunch Breaks

Under California law employees must be provided with no less than thirty minutes for a meal period if the work period is more than five hours (or six hours for those in the motion picture industry). The employee needs to be relieved of all duty during this meal period and be free to leave the premises. If not it would be considered "on duty," considered as time worked, and paid for at the employee's regular rate of pay. An unpaid "on duty" meal period is allowed if the nature of the work prevents the employee from being relieved of all duty if there's a written agreement between the employer and employee that is on-the-job meal period is acceptable.

Whether the nature of the work prevents an employee from being relieved of all duty is based on objective criteria. An employer and employee can't agree to an on duty meal period unless, based on objective criteria, any employee would be prevented from being relieved of all duty based on necessary job duties. Examples would be someone who interacts with the public alone or a lone security guard at a remote site.

The employer isn't required to make sure that no work is performed but the employer must not just simply make a meal period available. The employer must relieve employees of all duties, give up control over their activities, allow them a reasonable opportunity to take an uninterrupted thirty minute break, employees must be free to come and go and the employer can't impede or discourage employees from taking their meal period.

The employer can't undermine a policy of providing meal periods by pressuring employees to work in ways that omit breaks (like a break scheduling policy making breaks extremely difficult).

If someone works for a period of more than five hours, the meal period needs to be provided no later than the end of the fifth hour of work (or no later than the start of the sixth hour of work). If the employee works for more than ten hours, a second meal period must be provided no later than the end of the employee's tenth hour of work (no later than the start of the eleventh hour of work). These rules are subject to certain waivers by mutual consent and there are different rules for employees in the motion picture industry.

The employer need not pay for a meal period if there's bona fide relief from duty and giving up of employer control (and no discouragement or coercion from the employer against taking the meal period). If the employer knows, or has reason to know, an employee is working during an unpaid meal period, compensation is owed to the employee for the time worked (including overtime hours if applicable).

Overtime and Comp Time

Federal law requires that hourly employees be paid overtime for hours worked if they work more than forty hours in the week. Overtime must be paid at 1.5 times an employee's normal hourly rate. California requires overtime pay if the person worked more than eight hours in one day. Under federal labor law employers must include weekend hours with the time being worked during the rest of the week to calculate overtime. Exempt employees normally need not be paid overtime.

If an employee works more than eight hours a day, or more than forty hours in a work week, under California law the employer may need to pay overtime even if that extra work wasn't authorized by management. On the other hand an employer can require an employee to work overtime and failing to do so can be a reason for discipline.

Private employers aren't allowed to use comp time, or giving paid time off instead of paying overtime to hourly employees. California law has a number of exceptions to the general rules of overtime pay as well as how it may be applied to a particular classification of employee.

Flexible Schedules

State law generally requires overtime pay for all time worked in excess of eight hours per day and 40 hours per week. But one of the loopholes allows employers to adopt alternative work schedules where employees may work more than eight hours in a day without requiring the payment of overtime if the employer follows a special election procedure.

This alternative work schedule can be used if a two-thirds majority of employees in the affected "work unit" vote in favor of it. A work unit is a division, department, job classification, shift, separate physical location, or a recognized subdivision thereof. It could be an individual employee if these criteria are met.

Paycheck Deductions

Under California law an employer can withhold from an employee's wages when a deduction is,

- Required or allowed to do so by state or federal law (such as wage garnishment due to a debt or child support payments),

- Expressly authorized in writing by the employee to cover insurance premiums, benefit plan contributions or other deductions not amounting to a rebate on the employee's wages, or,

- Covering health, welfare, or pension contributions expressly authorized by a wage or collective bargaining agreement.

Some common payroll deductions are unlawful, including,

- Gratuities: An employer can't collect, take, or receive any gratuity, or part of it, given or left for an employee, or deduct from wages a gratuity given or left for an employee. A restaurant is allowed to pool or share tips among employees who provide direct table service to customers.
- The cost of a required photograph of the employee.
- The cost of a bond required by the employer.
- The cost of required uniforms. If an employer requires a uniform the employer must pay for it.
- Business expenses.
- Medical or physical examinations required of a job applicant.

A loan from an employer to an employee can be repaid through payroll deductions if it's authorized in writing by the employee. However, if by the employee's last paycheck more than the periodic payment is due, only the normally installment can be taken out. There can be no balloon payment in the last paycheck.

Vacation Pay

California law doesn't require that employees receive vacation pay. However, if the employer chooses vacation pay as part of an employee's compensation, there are restrictions on how the employer fulfills its obligations. Under California law earned vacation time is considered wages, and vacation time is earned, or vests, as labor is performed. Vacation pay accrues as it's earned, and cannot be lost, even if the employee is fired, no matter the reason why.

There can be a reasonable cap on vacation benefits to prevent an employee from earning vacation over a certain amount of hours. Unless it's agreed to in a collective bargaining agreement, when employment ends all earned and unused vacation must be paid to the employee at his or her final rate of pay so a "use it or lose it" vacation policy would be illegal under California law.

"When an employee is terminated, you are taking his/her income away, so handle it with care." - Tony T. Liu

---

How Do I Fire an Employee While Limiting the Chances of Being Sued?

No matter what steps you take or how conscientious you are when deciding to fire someone, there is no guarantee a lawsuit by a former employee will be avoided. However, if certain steps are taken and you develop a body of evidence that will support your contention no laws were broken, the easier, quicker and cheaper it may be to get a lawsuit dismissed.

When making a decision whether or not to fire an employee, you are dealing with their livelihood and you need to understand that letting a worker go means you have taken away their opportunity to earn income and, possibly, provide food for their families. Terminations are typically very emotionally charged. You must handle these issues as early as you can and with some understanding. The person, as terrible an employee he or she may be, is still a person who should be treated with respect.

"An employment handbook is a guide, a subset of policies and procedures that deal with employment issues, and it need to be updated on at least an annual basis." - Tony T. Liu

---

To handle employee discipline, up to and including terminations, correctly, you should follow your written policies and procedures. They should be contained in your employment handbook (see below), which should cover a wide range of issues beyond the fact employees' employment is "at will."

Your handbook should be a living, breathing documents that impacts your company and employees, so time will need to be spent amending and updating them, especially if you expect your employees to follow them.

Your employee handbook could be construed by a court as a binding contract and it's best an employer avoid that as much as possible. If it is seen as a contract a fired employee may claim the contract was violated because policies or procedures weren't followed as promised, causing harm to the ex-employee.

To try to avoid this,

- Include a clear, distinct, prominent statement the handbook is not a contract. Have the employee sign a receipt for the handbook clearly acknowledging it's just information and guidance, not a contract, and

- Don't include any language in the handbook essentially stating that if an employee does certain things or avoids doing certain things there will be job security.

The handbook should be regularly updated. If a policy isn't getting you the intended results, change it. If a court decision impacts a policy, you should update it. Circulate the changes as updates to the handbook.

Document, Document, Document.

Updated, effectively enforced policies and procedures (embodied in your handbook) are a good thing, but they will only get you so far if you are sued by an employee or ex-employee if the person is disciplined, demoted, given a pay cut or fired. During the discipline and performance evaluation process you need to follow these policies and procedures and document the quality of the person's work and any problems the person may have.

Documentation of problems put together after the decision to fire the person's been made or after you've been sued will probably not be seen as credible. Document performance in real time, as things happen.

If the quality and quantity of work can be documented, you should do so. Any breach of policies or procedures should also be documented, including the names of decision makers and any witnesses or co-workers who can corroborate the worker's problems. Any investigations into alleged wrongdoing by an employee should also be documented.

Litigation is like a gun fight. If you're going to be involved in one, do you want bullets in your gun or not? If in response to a lawsuit you have to resort to stating that there were rumors of something or management thought the person did or didn't do something or someone recalls a conversation without being able to produce notes of conversations or there are no documents establishing why you took certain actions, there are no bullets in your gun. Who do you think will be left standing after this gun fight?

Not only is there no corroborating, documented evidence to help you, the lack of such evidence will make you look less credible to a government agency, judge or jury. In this day and age if something went wrong in the workplace but it wasn't documented a fact finder may not believe it happened. Credibility is key to success when dealing with legal actions.

In employment discrimination cases it may be enough for a fact finder to find in favor of an employee or ex-employee simply because the employer's explanation isn't credible. If you want to be credible in a lawsuit or government complaint concerning an employee, you need to document your side of the story.

Discrimination Claims.

Under federal law it's generally illegal for an employer to fail to hire, fire or subject to unequal terms and conditions job applicants or employees based on their,

- Race,
- Color,
- National origin,
- Ethnicity,
- Religion,
- Sex (including pregnancy, childbirth, and related medical conditions),
- Disability,
- Age (40 and older),
- Opposition to discrimination, participation in the investigation or litigation of a discrimination claim, asking for or receiving a reasonable

accommodation to a disability or family medical leave (retaliation),

- Citizenship status,
- Genetic information, and,
- Complaint of illegal or unethical activities (whistleblower).

California law protects the same people and also prohibits discrimination based on,

- Marital status,
- Sexual orientation,
- Gender identity and gender expression,
- AIDS/HIV (though it would fall under disability in federal law),
- Medical condition,
- Political activities or affiliations,
- Military or veteran status, and,
- Status as a victim of domestic violence, assault or stalking.

If an employee falls into one of these classifications, he or she belongs to a "protected class."

Anti-discrimination laws not only cover employees because of what they are (sex, race, citizenship status) but also because of what they do. They're involved in what's called protected activity: they complain of discrimination, ask for (and/or receive) time off under the Family Medical Leave Act, ask for accommodations for a disability or report to a government agency a reasonable belief that you're engaging in fraud in a government contract (whistleblower).

Cities and counties may also have their own employment anti-discrimination laws. For example, height and weight are protected classes in San Francisco.

Discrimination general boils down something like...the plaintiff and others of the same protected class are treated worse than others of different classes. Latinos or women are disciplined more harshly than others committing the same or similar infraction or less qualified white job candidates are hired over more experienced African American job candidates.

The plaintiff has the burden of proof to show it's more likely than not the illegal discrimination took place. There are different ways to establish this proof.

- Direct evidence: There's evidence the decision maker showed an explicit bias against those of plaintiff's protected class through words, remarks or in writing.

- Indirect or comparative evidence: Through personnel records, testimony, copies of emails or memos the plaintiff can show a history of preferential treatment of one group of employees and/or a history of negative treatment of those in plaintiff's protected class.

- Disparate impact: While the other two cases require the plaintiff to show some kind of illegal intent to discriminate, this type of case does not. In these cases an apparently neutral rule or policy that when it's applied has a disparate impact on those of a certain protected class. Educational qualifications may screen out African Americans who otherwise would be able to do the job or a physical abilities test that doesn't accurately simulate the job of a firefighter may screen out female job applicants. These types of cases are the least common and most difficult to prove but can impact a large number of people.

Though sexual harassment has become more publicized and less socially acceptable after high profile allegations against the rich, powerful and famous, harassment is also illegal if it's based on any protected classes. Harassment becomes unlawful when,

- Enduring the offensive conduct becomes a condition of continued employment,
- The conduct is severe or pervasive enough to create a work environment that a reasonable person would consider intimidating, hostile or abusive, or,
- It results in a tangible action against the victim (pay cut, demotion, firing).

Depending on the facts of the situation and applicable laws there are many potential defenses to a discrimination complaint.

- If you have a genuine, effective, internal mechanism to investigate discrimination and harassment claims at your business and if those found to have discriminated or harassed others face discipline that fits the situation it may result in a discrimination claim being dismissed or may reduce potential damages.

- A lack of policies or procedures concerning addressing complaints, a nonexistent or sham investigation that doesn't take discrimination claims seriously or hold those responsible accountable won't do you any good when it comes to defending your business. It might actually make the situation worse because it could appear your business is more interested in covering up the problem than addressing it.

Accommodating Disabled Employees.

Under the federal Americans with Disabilities Act (ADA) and state law disabled employees need to be reasonably accommodated. What that accommodation should be depends on the needs of the employee and employer. That accommodation will probably be cheap, easy and not disrupt your operations.

But each case is unique and you may have a situation that's challenging. To qualify for an accommodation under the ADA the employee must have a substantial impairment of a major life activity while being able to perform the essential functions of a position. Businesses with fifteen or more employees fall under the ADA and those with five or more need to comply with state law, so if your business is small enough, these rules don't apply.

The employee is entitled to a reasonable accommodation that doesn't pose an undue hardship to the business. What may be reasonable and not a hardship for one business may not be reasonable and create an undue hardship for another. As part of the process you can ask your employee to get from his or her physician clarification as to what is needed.

Both sides need to engage in an interactive process to try to work something out. If you just say no to a disabled employee and cut off discussions about accommodations, you've violated the law. If an employee is just as intransigent and insists that only his or her proposal is the right one, any legal action by this employee would probably be dismissed because he or she shut down the interactive process. But don't string out the process indefinitely, rejecting one thing after another, instead of just saying no. This approach would also violate the ADA.

An employer should look at the situation as an exercise in creative problem solving. It may force you to look at the duties of a particular job and decide what functions are critical, important or can easily done by someone else or not done at all. This shouldn't be a battle of wills but a joint effort to see what can be done to keep an employee working and productive.

A "this is how we do things" approach could land you in trouble. Cases where employees have asked to be able to sit on stools (even just part of the time) instead of standing all day at cash registers or assembly lines have been litigated in federal court. Would you rather spend six figures to litigate whether or not an employee should sit part of the time or just buy some stools?

"Let's give it a try," is a great phrase for both sides to use in these situations. Maybe you have some doubts about the changes the employee wants and maybe the employee doubts what you want to do will be helpful. Choose a proposal and document the results. Is the employee doing OK or not? Has productivity been affected? Were any disruptions caused? Meet with the employee to see how things are going and make changes as necessary. If it's not working, try something else.

Pregnant Employees

An employer cannot fire, refuse to hire, demote or take any other adverse action against a woman if pregnancy, childbirth or a related medical condition was a motivating factor in the decision, under the federal Pregnancy Discrimination Act (PDA). It prohibits discrimination concerning all aspects of employment, including pay, job assignments, promotions, layoffs, training and fringe benefits.

The PDA covers treatment based on an employee's fertility or childbearing capacity, pregnancy related issues that may arise after the pregnancy is over and the fact the employee was pregnant in the past.

Sex-specific policies preventing women from jobs based on childbearing capacity (such as those prohibiting women who may become pregnant from jobs with exposure to toxic chemicals) are generally prohibited. A sex-specific job restriction would only be justified if the employer can show that lack of childbearing capacity is a bona fide occupational qualification that's reasonably necessary to the normal operation of the business.

It would violate the PDA if an employer discriminates against an employee because she indicates she intends to become pregnant in the future. Though, strictly speaking, asking an employee or job applicant whether she is pregnant or if she intends to become pregnant doesn't violate federal law, the fact such a questions was asked may be used as evidence of an illegal bias against women.

If an employee is temporarily disabled because of a pregnancy she needs to be treated just as well as other employees with temporary disabilities or you violate the PDA. If you offer light duty work to those injured on the job you should do the same for your pregnant employees. If you have double standards in your workplace and an employee temporarily disabled due to a pregnancy gets the short end of the stick, you may be inviting a lawsuit.

If a pregnant employee suffers from a long term or permanent disability that meets the requirements of the federal ADA or state discrimination laws, they could apply as well. An employee may also have rights to a leave under federal and state family medical leave laws.

Libel and Defamation.

If you make false, damaging statements about a current or former employee and that employee suffers harm as a result, that person may be able to maintain a legal action against your company.

Libel happens when the statement is in writing, defamation when the statement is spoken. Either way the statement must be published, it was heard or seen by someone other than the originator.

Often in employment situations an employee leaves your company or is fired, he or she applies for another job and as part of the hiring process you are contacted. Making a damaging statement that results in the person not getting hired (and suffering monetary damages) may result in a lawsuit against you. If so, the issue may be whether or not your statement is true (which is an absolute defense) or not (which could create liability).

Many employers avoid this by only giving neutral references such as the person's position, dates of employment and rate of pay. If the person's departure from the company is contentious, possibly including legal claims by the employee against you, part of a resolution of the matter could include a letter of reference whose language is agreed to by both parties.

A Lawsuit May be the Least of Your Worries.

Workplace violence is violence or the threat of violence against workers, according to the federal Occupational Safety and Health Administration (OSHA). It can happen at your business and can be anything from harassment and intimidation to threats, physical assaults and homicide.

- It's been estimated that workplace violence incidents have tripled in the last decade.
- It's now the fastest growing category of murder in the U.S.
- The situation has gotten so bad that the U.S. Department of Justice declared the workplace as one of the most dangerous places to be.
- About two million U.S. workers are victims of workplace violence annually, according to OSHA.

Generally, workplace violence occurs because of issues within the employer or a spouse, ex-spouse, partner, ex-partner or family member comes to the workplace to confront an employee because of their relationship. It's been an estimated that a quarter of American women have dealt with domestic violence and murder by domestic abusers is the leading killer of women in the workplace.

You can take steps to protect an employee from domestic violence. You could inform your workforce that if they fear someone may come to the workplace to harm them, or if they've obtained a court order prohibiting the person to come near them (including at their workplace), you should be informed of the situation.

The employee could provide the person's name and photo so if the person is seen or comes into the workplace, the affected employee could be warned and the police called. This could be especially helpful if you have a reception area and limited access to the workplace. If your business is open to the public, like a retail business, what you can do is limited, but do the best you can. Anyone going through this situation needs all the help he or she can get.

Often employees or ex-employees who perpetrate workplace violence claim that they've been treated unfairly or were disrespected by management or co-workers and they struck back. Business owners and management should not engage in or tolerate harassment, bullying or disrespectful behavior of one employee, or a group of employees, by other employees. Not only might you be sued if you participate in or allow these behaviors, you may be sowing the seeds of violence involving your employees.

Violence may also be sparked by discipline or a termination. Though the risk of this will result in violence is small, the potential harm that could result is great. Disciplining your employees in a systematic, logical, documented, fair way can reduce the chances of violence in your workplace.

If you think the situation may get out of hand you could have the employee escorted out the building after the termination, but this public humiliation may wind up the person even more and invoke a reaction later on.

You could be the most caring, empathetic, positive employer and still have violence occur in your workplace. Whether it's because of mental illness, addiction, family issues or some other profound source of stress in the person's life, the employee may lash out after getting bad news or a perceived slight from another employee.

But fostering an atmosphere of respect and fairness may help you reduce the chances of workplace violence happening in addition to lessening turnover, making it a place where people want to work and make it easier for you to attract new, qualified, motivated employees.

Properly handling employees is one of the greatest challenges a business faces. You want to get the most from your workforce but without driving employees away because they feel like cogs in a machine, not human being with something to contribute and who deserve respect.

On the other hand you need to control your workforce in order to control your business. There are many laws impacting the employee-employer relationship and taking actions without knowing the applicable laws or getting counsel from an attorney can turn a problem with an employee to a major challenge facing your business. Employment related legal actions and government investigations not only can drain you of financial resources but also time and energy you need to run your business.

There is no lack of legal actions filed against businesses due to employees or former employees who don't have all the facts, have emotions that aren't justified by the actual situation or they seek revenge for a perceived injustice. You may suffer one in the future, but you should do your best to comply with the law and reduce the chances employment related legal issues will set you and your business back.

Mistake No. 4
Not Protecting Intellectual Properties or Trade Secrets.

The fourth legal mistake that small business owners make is not protecting their intellectual property or trade secrets. This may be the most important and valuable assets a company may have.

Your company has many valuable assets. You may have a lot of inventory, equipment, vehicles, computers or servers. Do you have security systems, locks and keys to prevent them from being stolen? If you do, it's because these measures of protection are much cheaper than the cost of replacement.

Other valuable assets includes information, your plans and data. Taking steps to prevent them from being lost or stolen are also much cheaper than the cost of replacement and damage than can be done to your company by others. You need to protect your intellectual property and trade secrets because their loss could be very costly, if not crippling, to your business.

You should protect your intellectual property (IP) sooner than later.

- You may see this as non-essential because it's not legally required to operate your business or there seem to be more practical ways to spend your time and money that appear to be more pressing.

- If you're starting a new business or have come up with a new product or service you may be unsure whether the business, product or service will be successful. You might fear your investment in the process might not be worth it.

- You may not anticipate someone trying to copy your idea.

- You may not know what types of legal protections may be available for your products or brands.

- You may try to keep costs down by using free or inexpensive online resources.

If this is how you're thinking or acting, this is very short sighted and may end up costing you much, much more money than you think you need to invest to protect your IP and trade secrets.

Protecting IP correctly is not always simple, and many times the examining attorneys at the government agencies have questions or raise unexpected issues on the applications. That is why professional help is so important. It can be costly or limiting in the long run to skip these steps. I have worked with clients who wished they had taken protective steps sooner.

The Basics-Types of IP Protections

This could be customer lists, marketing plans, recipes or formulas. They are key to the business' daily function and its future success.

IP rights are like any other property right. They allow creators, or owners, of patents, trademarks or copyrighted works to benefit from their own work or investment in a creation.

There are several things you can do to protect your IP. They involve getting protection through state and federal law (trademarks, copyrights, patents and trade secret protections) as well as actions you can take to minimize the risk of loss.

Patents

A patent is an exclusive right granted for an invention (a product or process that provides a new way of doing something, or that offers a new technical solution to a problem). They are licenses that the government issues to you (through the U.S. Patent and Trademark Office (USPTO)) for the exclusive use of an invention for a period of time (generally up to 20 years). The purpose of patents is to promote the invention or innovation and encourage its development and sale.

Patent protection gives the holder the ability to control who can make it. The holder can use it to help his or her own business or license others, for a fee, to exploit it. Patent rights are usually enforced in federal court but a court can also declare a patent invalid upon a successful challenge by a third party.

Owners may also sell their invention rights to someone else, who then becomes the new owner of the patent. Once a patent expires, protection ends and the invention enters the public domain

Do you want or need a patent? A patent is a valuable tool, but it may or may not be right for you and your business. Before investing in a patent application, you need to decide if it's a smart business decision.

Is your idea a viable business opportunity? You need to understand your product, the target market and the competition in the marketplace. Do your homework so you won't spend time, energy and money developing a product and seeking a patent application without a firm basis in believing it will be profitable.

You should,

- Perform patent research: Has this already been patented? Will your product infringe on someone else's patent? You can hire an expert to perform this research to do this or try it yourself.

- Create a prototype: Put together a basic prototype to see how functional it will be. This way your design will be as close to final design as possible when filing for the patent.

- Perform market research: What's your market and how big is it? Is it large enough for your product to be commercially viable?

- Cost to manufacture: How much it will cost to make your product? Whether you plan on selling or licensing the patent to others or making the product yourself, if the cost is greater than what the market will be willing to pay, there's no point in going forward.

If all this research points to a viable product, do you want or need a patent? Is a much less expensive trademark or copyright a viable option? Are you willing to run the risks of going without a patent in exchange for the lower upfront costs?

The benefits of a patent include,

- If you're going to make and sell the product yourself a patent can help you justify your investment in design, production and marketing. You'll have lead time over those who might copy your product, or at least come up with an alternative. You'll also have peace of mind that your invention is protected by law and that this protection can be enforced if someone infringes on your rights.

- If you want to license or sell your product to another company, you've reduced the prospective company's upfront legal costs and risks, justifying a higher royalty payment. The other party may feel secure the product won't infringe on other patents and you should feel at least a little more secure that if the company you're working with steals your design, your patent rights can be a basis to sue the other company.

There are also drawbacks to the patent process.

- The patent won't defend itself. It offers only the legal rights you're willing and able to enforce. There are no third parties looking out for your interests. If someone infringes on your patent, you'll need to spend time and money addressing the problem.

- If your product can be easily pulled apart and copied you may have to deal with several parties infringing your patent at the same time. Are you willing and able to do that?

- Patent claims can be very specific so it may not be hard to legally design a similar product.

If you don't have the resources to fully defend your product you may want to patent it but then license or sell your rights to another party who does.

If you decide a patent is right for you and your business, to be eligible for a patent an invention must,

- Be of practical use,

- Show an element of "novelty" (some new characteristic that is not part of the body of existing knowledge in its particular technical field, or "prior art"),

- Show an "inventive step" that could not be deduced by a person with average knowledge of the technical field, and

- Its subject matter must be "patentable" under law.

If you invent something or you create a design or manufacturing process speak with a patent attorney. This area is highly specialized and very technical. Only patent attorneys can advise you about whether your particular idea or invention is patentable.

Trademark

A trademark is a distinctive sign identifying certain goods or services are produced or provided by a given individual or a company. The system helps consumers identify and purchase a product or service based on its unique, identifying brand.

Trademark protection ensures that the owners of these marks have the exclusive right to use them to identify goods or services, or to allow others to use them in return for payment. The period of protection varies, but a trademark can be renewed indefinitely upon payment of the corresponding fees. Trademark protection is legally enforced by the court system which has the authority to stop trademark infringement.

Trademarks also promote initiative and enterprise worldwide by rewarding their owners with recognition and financial profit. Trademark protection also hinders the efforts of unfair competitors, such as counterfeiters, to use the same or similar marks to sell inferior or different products or services.

Trademarks can be one or a combination of words, letters and numerals. They may consist of drawings, symbols or three-dimensional signs, such as the shape and packaging of goods.

A trademark need not be registered and as long as you use your trademark consistently, you are the owner. However, you gain extra protection if you register your trademarks with the USPTO because it will be easier for you to prove your ownership of it someone else uses, or wants to use it, in the future.

Copyright

Copyright laws grant authors, artists and other creators protection for their literary and artistic creations, referred to as "works." The creators of works protected by copyright, and their heirs and successors ("right holders"), have certain basic rights under copyright law. They have the exclusive right to use or authorize others to use the work. The right holder(s) of a work can authorize or prohibit the work being performed or published in a number of ways.

Copyright protection covers the creation of creative works, such as songs, books, designs, art and even software. Like trademarks, you do not need to register copyrights to establish your ownership of them. However, you must be consistent in your use of these copyrights and you must be able to prove that you are the owners of the copyright.

If you register your copyrights with the USPTO, you gain extra protection and it's easier for you to establish or prove your ownership of the copyright in court.

Common Intellectual Property Issues for Small Business Owners

They are,

- Brand name research,
- Brand name protection,
- Confidentiality and trade secrets, and,
- Non-compete and non-disclosure agreements.

Brand Name Research

To ensure that the brand name you want for your business isn't the same or too similar to an existing brand name or trademark in your market you need to see if others are using. Do your own name availability search before you start the process of trademarking. Generally, if someone is using the brand before you do, they have the rights to it, you don't, so investing time, energy and money into that brand could be a huge waste.

You can conduct a preliminary online search for the name. Enter your desired name plus ".com" in the address line of your web browser. Is there such a website? You may also want to enter the name into different search engines to see if businesses with your desired name appear in the search results.

Search California's database of registered business names. This database is maintained by Secretary of State. You should also screen the name with the USPTO, which keeps a database of pending, registered and expired federal trademarks.

If another business is using the name you want, you may be able to use it if your market area or industry doesn't overlap with that of the other business. However, doing so may risk legal action by the other party, claiming you're causing marketplace confusion by giving your brand the same name as another business' brand.

Protect Your Brand!

When you started your company, you created a name you wanted to brand because it reflects your culture, values and the things you want to do. You will spend a significant amount of time, energy and money creating, spreading, protecting and reinforcing this brand.

You are in business because you have a great idea. Then, you create names, symbols and unique designs for your company so consumers will not confuse your products or services with those from a competitor.

Take the effort to protect your intellectual property. Otherwise, you are going to lose it.

Actions you can take to protect your brand include,

- Trademarking your brand name.

- Police your mark: Even if your brand is trademarked you may lose your rights to it if others are freely using it without any consequences. Check the internet periodically if anyone else comes up who's using your mark.

- Send 'Take Down' notices: If you find another party using your mark without authorization, it can be sent a "Cease and Desist" letter, or a "Take Down Notice." This puts that party on notice that you're aware of what they're doing, you own the mark and they're required by law to remove any infringements from their websites, servers, products or services. Failing to defend your trademark rights may result in you losing those rights, especially if your trademark isn't registered with the USPTO.

Protect Your Confidential Information and Trade Secrets

"Trade Secret-if it is a secret, treat it like one. If you don't, it is not a secret." - Tony T. Liu

---

Trade secrets are proprietary information you have but others do not. A court will consider a number of factors to determine whether specific company information is a trade secret and worthy of legal protection.

One is whether or not you're taking actions to protect them. If you want the court to look at this information as if it is a secret, you better treat it like one. If you do not have a policy or procedure for protecting this information and you let everybody in your company have access to it, then it's not a secret.

The recipe for Coca-Cola is a classic example of a trade secret. I have heard that only two people within the company know the recipe for the original Coca-Cola. The amount of effort the company expends to protect the formula is incredible. For nearly 100 years, only two people have known the recipe or formula. This kind of secrecy shows the court that Coke is serious about its trade secrets.

Internal company information is not a trade secret. You must make the effort to protect your trade secrets through a policy and procedure, a safeguard, or by limiting access to the information to a certain person or persons. Only key employees should have access to trade secrets.

Many business owners think their client lists are trade secrets. They may or may not, depending on the circumstances. I do not believe customer lists are considered trade secrets in California. However, the court will look into the amount you spent (such as $250,000 or $500,000 over three or four years) to develop the list before it will consider the list to be a trade secret, generally speaking.

This information may be confidential within your company, but it may not be considered a trade secret by the court. Unfortunately, with the power of internet, your information may be available to everybody. There are always exceptions, so consult with attorney and go over your issues in detail to make that determination.

The California Uniform Trade Secrets Act (UTSA) provides protections for trade secrets and creates liability for those who misappropriate them. As long as a company takes reasonable measures to protect its trade secrets, and if the information is valuable because it's kept secret, California courts will recognize that seemingly common, every-day pieces of data can be afforded legal protection as a trade secret potentially punishing others for their disclosure.

UTSA doesn't use "theft" as one of its terms, it uses something more genteel, "misappropriation." It includes two types of misuse: the acquisition by improper means and the use or disclosure of trade secrets.

- "Improper means" includes "theft, bribery, misrepresentation, breach or inducement of a breach of duty to maintain secrecy or espionage through electronic or other means." Civil Code section 3426.1(a). If a former employee decides to work for a competitor and takes or copies a trade secret (like a marketing plan) and carries it away in a thumb drive or emails it to his personal email account or that of his new employer, that information would be acquired by improper means.

- The second definition of "misappropriation" includes the prohibition of the use or disclosure of trade secret information. A former employee's use or disclosure of confidential customer information to solicit new accounts on for a new employer would be considered the misappropriation of a trade secret.

These trade secrets need not be in a physical or electronic form when used or taken by the other party. Under the UTSA a plaintiff need not show the former employee physically took trade secret information. The law also covers the contents of an employee's memory, as long as the information fits the definition of a trade secret. A company could show the employee used or disclosed the contents of his or her memories regarding a trade secret to establish a misappropriation happened.

Simply showing the employee remembered trade secrets and worked elsewhere won't be enough to win a case. Courts have placed limits on relying on the employee's memory to base a misappropriation claim. A plaintiff could try to prevent the employee from taking the job because the former employee will inevitably disclose the former employer's trade secrets. California courts have rejected this "inevitable disclosure doctrine" and they require evidence of use or disclosure be presented in order to maintain a legal claim. The former employer needs evidence of the use or disclosure of trade secret information before filing a lawsuit.

What do you need to show to establish liability for your competitor after it hires your employee whose head, if not his thumb drive, is filled with trade secrets? It may claim it didn't know its new employee had used or disclosed trade secret information. Under the UTSA the standard a plaintiff must pass to establish liability is not actual knowledge of wrongdoing, but constructive knowledge (the facts show the company's principals knew or should have known that the alleged wrongdoing was occurring).

To be protected by the USTA your company needs to take reasonable measures to protect its trade secret information. This includes,

- Electronic measures such as using secured networks, limited employee access, firewalls, multi-character passwords, or other ways to limit access or to track employee network activity.

- Employee handbooks should clearly state sharing of trade secrets is forbidden and could result in termination.

- If the information is maintained on paper or in a physical form such as a CD-ROM, access to it should be physically restricted such as keeping it in a locked file. Those using it may need to sign it in and out.

These measures will help you establish the information fits the legal definition of a trade secret (you're making efforts to restrict access to it) and discourage misappropriation because it's difficult to access the information. They also might be able to provide evidence as to who took the information or who was aware of it.

Other steps a business can take include,

- Ensuring there are contractual obligations in place to protect confidential data and trade secrets. Employees, or at least those with access to trade secrets, should sign confidentiality agreements explicitly stating they won't take or use elsewhere your trade secrets or solicit your current or past customers. Confidentiality agreements should also be signed by contractors with access to your trade secrets.

- Creating policies covering the use of electronic storage devices, internet use and use of the company's e-mail system to try to prevent misappropriation.

- Reminding employees of their contractual obligations to protect confidential information and not to use or disclose trade secrets. This can be covered when a person is hired and during an exit interviews. A certified letter to an ex-employee's last known address containing a reminder is also a good idea.

- Having a plan of action in case you learn your trade secrets have been misappropriated or if you hired someone who may have misappropriated the trade secrets of others.

It's not just former employees who may be spilling your trade secrets beans. You may be doing it to without really realizing it. You want to create a joint venture with or sell your business to Company A. You have certain knowledge, copyrights and confidential information (trade secrets) that will need to be shared in the course of the other company doing its "due diligence."

After the preliminary discussions are over and it's time to get serious, the parties should sign a non-compete agreement and confidentiality agreement because confidential information and knowledge (trade secrets) will be discussed to facilitate the joint venture process and work relationship. These agreements prevent either company from disclosing this information to a third party, or, with the benefit of this information, prevent Company A to have an advantage over you if the proposed joint venture never happens or ends in the future.

Noncompete Agreements

You might think one way to try to protect your intellectual property and trade secrets is to have a noncompete agreement made between your company and an employee. Good idea but these non-compete agreements are rarely enforceable under California law, unless they involve high level management employees, which are enforceable on a case by case basis. Most of the time non-compete agreements with employees are not enforceable.

If the non-compete agreement is made between the business partners in a joint venture situation, two key requirements must be met,

- The time and geographic scope of the agreement must be reasonable. One or two years might be deemed reasonable, but time provisions differ by state.

- If the geographic scope is the entire world, it's unlikely the agreement would be enforceable. If it's limited to the State of California, but allows you to use the ideas outside of California, the agreement may be enforceable. Be specific. If you don't want to compete with a company in Southern California, your agreement should list whatever counties in the region you want just to yourself.

If you are in California, call our office, and we will advise you about whether your agreement is enforceable and whether the scope of your geographic limitation is reasonable. If you are outside of California, consult with a local attorney about the state laws that are applicable in your situation.

Non-Disclosure Agreements (NDA's)

These agreements can help keep your trade secrets and intellectual property confidential. They should not only be signed by employees but any contractor, supplier and any company with which you do business, have a joint venture or are in negotiations with concerning a sale of your business.

The purpose of an NDA is to create a confidential relationship between the person or entity with a trade secret and the person or entity to whom the secret is shared. People and entities in such a relationship are legally bound to keep the information a secret.

A confidential relationship can also be created through an oral agreement or it can be implied from the conduct of the parties. You don't want to go either of these routes because, like any oral contract, they're much more difficult to prove. If it's not in writing there can be competing and contradictory testimony, not something you normally have to deal with if the relationship is based on a written agreement.

There are five basic parts to an NDA,

- Definition of confidential information,
- Exclusions from confidential information,
- Obligations of the receiving party,
- Applicable time periods, and,
- Miscellaneous provisions.

There should be a list of the types or categories of confidential information to be protected. This establishes the boundaries, or the subject matter, of the disclosure, without actually disclosing the secrets (such as "Confidential information includes programming code, financial information, related software materials, and innovative processes.").

As part of setting boundaries there are also exclusions. Exclusions state the party getting the excluded information is not obligated to protect it. Exceptions are based on established principles of law, including information that was created or discovered by the receiving party before, or independent of, any involvement with the disclosing party.

The obligations of the receiving party normally states it needs to hold and maintain the information in confidence and limit its use. The receiving party agrees not to breach the confidential relationship, induce others to breach it, or induce others to acquire the secret by improper means.

The time period depends on the parties. This is the given time frame the information needs to be kept confidential.

Miscellaneous provisions can include damages and fees available to the party harmed by the agreement's breach, under what state law disputes would be adjudicated and whether arbitration is required if a party feels the agreement's been breached.

We are in the information or digital age. Even if your business is in manufacturing or you distribute or sell products, you should understand how critical information is to your business. Taking steps to try to prevent its loss will be far less costly than coping with the potential damage suffered due to its loss and getting involved in legal actions to chase down those who broke the law and harmed your business.

Mistake No. 5 - Bad Judgement

It's perfectly understandable that you want to run a business as you see fit, making as much profit as possible. You run a business, not a charity, and this is the free market system. You have many competitors and none will shed a tear if you close up shop.

That being said, cutting legal corners or just doing things that are illegal, in order to make your life easier or your business more profitable is a mistake. It may work for a while but eventually this will catch up to you. Depending on what you did, this could cost you a lot of money (possibly enough to threaten your business), create huge public relations problems, ruin your reputation, result in your clients and customers going elsewhere and you might end up in jail.

Part of being an attorney is representing business owners who are in this situation and if you've gotten yourself into trouble a good attorney will do all he or she can to limit the damage and help you get the best possible outcome. But given all you've done to create opportunities for your business and your family, this is the last place you want to be. It's much easier and cheaper not to create a legal problem than it is to try to solve it.

You may find yourself in the position where you're tempted to do something not quite kosher, something you think will help your business but it's a little shady. Your business may not be doing well and you could use a little help. You might think there's a small chance it will come to light in the future so you decide to go for it.

Many otherwise honest and respectable business owners find themselves in this position. Before they know it as a result of one bad decision, they need to do something else that's questionable. Then the issue comes up again and they either need to admit their mistakes and face the consequences or, in order to help keep it quiet longer, engage in fraud or deceit. This is a slippery slope you don't want to be on.

In addition to the issues we've already covered there are many others, large and small, that can cost you your credibility, result in being on the losing end of a lawsuit, threaten your business and land you in jail if you use bad judgement.

Fraud

Business fraud often takes place when management has confidential information or access to sensitive assets, then takes advantage of those assets or information for a gain. The fraud is behind the appearance of legitimate business practices in order to disguise the illegal activity.

The accounting of a company's assets may be changed to show what appears to be high revenue and profits, while the reality is much different. Management might want to hide net losses, slow revenue, declining sales or high expenses. These cooked books might be used to make the company more attractive to potential buyers, lenders and investors.

Other forms of corporate fraud may try to disguise or misrepresent a current or future service or product to hide its flaws or defects. Instead of repairing, refurbishing or redesigning the product, management tries to deflect or disguise these issues. The company may not have enough money or other resources to correct the problem or revealing the issue might drive away customers and investors. Management may think continuing the charade is more profitable than ending it.

A company claiming it's using some of its funds to put towards investments or other types of monetary reserves supposedly intended to gain in value, but those funds are spent or diverted elsewhere is engaging in fraud.

Fraud can also involve the false representation of facts by intentionally withholding important information or using false statements to another party in order to obtain something that may not have been provided without the deception.

Management may be aware of information that the intended victim is not, allowing management to deceive and defraud the victim. The company is taking advantage of the fact it has information the victim does not. The cost of reviewing and verifying given information is true and complete can be high enough to discourage the victim from doing more to verify the story. An insurance company may pay off a small claim because of what it sees as a small chance of fraud and the costs of fully verifying the loss.

California and federal law criminalize fraud, though fraud may not always result in a criminal trial. Government prosecutors have a lot of discretion in deciding if a case should go to trial and may pursue a plea bargain instead. If a fraud case goes to trial, the perpetrator may be convicted and sent to jail.

Whether or not there's a criminal prosecution those harmed by the fraud may sue the company in civil court. The victims may sue to have funds recovered, or, if there was no monetary loss, they may sue to reestablish their legal rights to something.

Proving fraud was committed in civil court requires a showing the defendant committed specific acts.

- It provided a false statement of material fact or it had an obligation to disclose certain information and chose not to do so.
- The defendant knew that the statement was false.
- The defendant intended to deceive the plaintiff.
- The plaintiff can show it relied on the false or missing statement.

- The victim suffered damages because of its reliance on the intentionally false or missing statement.

Securities Fraud

Securities fraud is a "white collar" crime that can be committed in a number of ways but normally includes misrepresenting information investors use to make decisions.

The perpetrator can be an individual, like a stockbroker, or a business or bank. These types of fraud can be a high yield investment fraud, Ponzi schemes or pyramid schemes. The party committing the fraud seeks to deceive investors by misrepresentation. It can involve providing false information, withholding key information, intentionally offering bad advice and offering or acting on inside information.

Securities fraud is limited only by the imagination of the perpetrator. It may involve promises of high returns by little risk. The investments may be commodities, securities or real estate. Ponzi and pyramid schemes take funds provided by new investors to pay the returns that were promised to prior investors caught up in the arrangement. The scheme lasts only as long as new investors/victims can be recruited because there normally is little or no actual investments being made. Securities fraud can carry criminal and civil penalties by the federal Securities and Exchange Commission, resulting in imprisonment and fines, along with civil lawsuits by victims.

Marketing Fraud

Marketing fraud is illegal practices perpetrated by a company to promote a product or service. This usually includes making false claims about the quality or value of what's being marketed, selling imitations as the genuine article, or hiding negative aspects or side effects.

Normally if a company makes a product that injures someone business insurance should cover such a claim. However, if there is such a lawsuit and an insurance company believes the manufacturer or seller made false statements about its quality or safety it may deny coverage of the claim, leaving the company exposed to what could be very expensive litigation.

Contractor Fraud

Contractor fraud is illegal business practices committed by companies hired to renovate, repair or build buildings or properties. It's often done by smaller firms promising quick repairs or upgrades at below market prices. The work is often substandard, unnecessary, may cause damage to parts of the building and create a safety hazard. The victim may be pressured into paying for the work up front.

Contractor fraud costs the victim twice because they pay for substandard or nonexistent work then pay someone else to do it right. As with marketing fraud if someone is injured because of substandard work or work that wasn't done, the contractor's insurance carrier may deny a claim to cover the injury, exposing the contractor to a personal injury lawsuit.

Tax Fraud

Tax fraud occurs when an individual or business entity intentionally falsifies information on a tax return or other documents to limit the company's tax liability or receive a refund it doesn't deserve. Management could claim false or inflated deductions and not report, or under report, income. This can involve local, state or federal taxes. If caught a business could be forced to pay what it actually owed, plus interest and penalties, fines and possible jail time for the individual responsible.

Insurance Fraud

Insurance fraud occurs when someone knowingly lies to obtain an insurance benefit or a lower premium to which they are not otherwise entitled. It's a crime and could be prosecuted by the California Department of Insurance as a felony. The punishment for committing insurance fraud ranges from probation, fines, community service, restitution, confinement in county jail and/or state prison. There could also be federal prosecution and lawsuits by the affected insurance company to recoup money obtained through fraud.

Insurance fraud can be prosecuted when,

- The suspect intended to defraud the insurer.
- An act is completed.

- Just making a misrepresentation to an insurer with knowledge it's untrue is sufficient.
- The act and intent must come together.
- Actual loss need not be shown if the suspect commits an act with the intent to defraud.

There are many ways a business can commit insurance fraud.

- Making false statements about the number of employees and/or their duties in order to obtain lower workers compensation premiums.
- Arson or the intentional destruction of property or insured equipment while claiming losses were accidental in order to obtain cash through a claim.
- Selling property, company owned vehicles or inventory then claiming they were stolen.
- There may be actual damage or theft but the business inflates the value to file a larger claim or states a false reason for the damage or destruction to obtain insurance coverage.

No matter the type of fraud, management convinces itself it's better off committing fraud and will be more profitable keeping it up. Not in these calculation is the costs of civil litigation, investigations by government agencies and, depending on this issue, criminal prosecution.

Breaching Your Fiduciary Duties as a Board Member, Officer or Shareholder

If you're on the board of directors of a corporation or a corporate officer you have a fiduciary obligation to the corporation and its shareholders that mandates you act in good faith, use your best judgment and do your best to promote the corporation's interests. These obligations are known as an officer or director's fiduciary duty. It's created by the legal relationship between the individual and the corporation or shareholder.

These obligations under California law fall generally into two duties, the duty of loyalty and the duty of care.

- The duty of loyalty requires a corporate officer or director to always act in the corporation's best interest and he or she must avoid engaging in "self-dealing." This is conduct is actions by which a corporate officer or director takes advantage of his or her position in the corporation to benefit his or her own interests, not those of the corporation or shareholders. If an officer or director discloses a potential conflict of interest (like a partial ownership of a business that may enter into a contract with the corporation), recuses himself from any actions involving the conflict but the corporation decides to go ahead anyway, he or she hasn't violated his or her fiduciary obligations.

- The duty of care means that a corporate officer or director needs to carry out his or her duties at least as well as any ordinarily prudent person in similar circumstances. This can include failing to investigate and do due diligence research into a potential joint venture and partner. If such research would've found the potential partner lacks the finances or expertise to perform its side of the deal, the board member or officer breached the duty of care.

California has adopted the Business Judgment Rule. It states that there's a presumption a corporate director, in the performance of his or her duties, acts in accordance with the duties of care and loyalty.

- This rule protects directors from personal liability from breaching their fiduciary duties if they're acting in accordance with the state's California Corporations Code, and,

- The rule prevents a court from getting involved in management decisions made by directors in good faith and with the belief the action is the company's best interest.

In a closely held corporation whose shares aren't publicly traded, minority shareholders are vulnerable to majority shareholder oppression. This is marginalizing minority shareholders by managing and controlling the corporation by electing themselves, family members or friends as directors and officers. Once elected, they take actions about management, employment, compensation, dividends and other actions which lead to the "freezing out" of the minority owners. Because of these potential problems directors and officers in closely held corporations are generally held to higher fiduciary duties.

If you're a board member or officer in a corporation or a shareholder of a closely held corporation you need to use good judgement to avoid breaching your fiduciary duties. Depending on the situation the right choice on how to proceed may be obvious or not so clear. If you're unsure how to handle a situation, contact an attorney to discuss the situation, your obligations and your best options. It's important to discuss these situations to avoid potential problems that can break a business apart from the inside.

Libel and Defamation

You may be tempted to help bring your company up by pushing your competition down. That's all well and good, as long as it's done in an honest, legitimate way. Once you start making false statements you open yourself up to potential liability.

A good reputation is critical to the success of any business and it may have taken years to develop. False, negative, damaging statements by one business about another's products of services can be the basis of a legal action. Trade libel is considered a type of defamation and is considered defamatory statements about a business or the quality of a business's services or products.

Defamation occurs when a person makes false statements that are damaging to a party's reputation. Libel is a defamatory, written, statement and if the false, damaging statement is spoken it's considered slander. Either way if your company is sued because another company claims you made such statements, the plaintiff needs to show,

- You made a false statement of fact, not opinion, about the quality of the plaintiff's products or services,
- It was published (more than one person saw it),
- The statement was not true,
- It caused a monetary loss to the plaintiff, and
- The statement isn't considered privileged under the law.

A major part of marketing your company is showing that you, your products and services are better than the competition. If you go too far with that and make false statements, legal action may follow.

Commercial Disparagement

While trade libel and defamation cover statements about products of services, commercial disparagement involves statements about a business.

Commercial disparagement, also called business disparagement, occurs when derogatory statements are made about a business or a person's title to his or her property with the intent of discouraging others from dealing with the person or business. This can include statements that the business is dishonest, unethical or incompetent.

If you are accused of making such a statement and sued, the plaintiff must show,

- The statement is false,
- It was published,
- You intended, or reasonably believed, the statement would cause a financial loss for the plaintiff,
- A financial loss was, in fact, suffered (customers left and/or the statement discouraged new ones), and,
- You made it knowing that it's false or with reckless disregard of whether the statement is true or false.

In the heat of competition for customers or new employees you may be tempted to stretch the truth and state false things about another company. If the other company suffers as a result and learns about your statements your company may find itself being served with a lawsuit.

Violating Environment Protection Laws

There are many ways a business needs to comply with environmental protections laws. You need not be a multi-national chemical company or own a petroleum refinery to run afoul of these laws, which can be enforced by state and federal agencies and the subject of lawsuits if others are impacted.

Important environmental issues affecting business include disposal of industrial waste, water and air emissions. Laws may mandate businesses to buy or update equipment and procedures to meet imposed standards, which costs money. While some businesses may see this as a way to preserve the environment and "do the right thing" and build their brand as a nature-friendly company, others may see these requirements as too costly and not comply.

Businesses that manufacture products usually produce some kind of waste, including toxic waste whose release is regulated by the law. Whether toxic wastes are produced and if so, how much, vary from business to business. Permits may be needed to legal release these chemicals into the air or water. A business may be tempted to understate the types or amounts of toxics involved or once a permit is obtained, throw in additional chemicals.

You may want to expand your business but part of your property is on the wet side. It might even be considered a wetland, but you could really use the property. Hiring someone to fill in the area in order to build on it, without going through the proper process and getting the proper permits, would violate the law can could result in lawsuits from neighbors who suddenly find their properties under water that should be contained on your property.

Depending on the law being violated fines could range from hundreds to hundreds of thousands of dollars, the costs of cleaning up the mess you created and possible criminal prosecution.

Kickbacks or Commercial Bribery

A kickback is a type of bribery which is negotiated between two parties. In a kickback, one person accepts to be paid for a service on a quid pro quo basis (one action in exchange for a reciprocal action). Normally, the benefit (money, goods or services) is discussed ahead of time. Normally the two parties are cooperating, one isn't extorting the bribe from the other.

A company desperate to make a sale may offer the person representing a potential, off the books, unofficial "sweetener" to the deal. In exchange for the approval of the sale the person is provided cash or "gifts" of products, services maybe a vacation or an envelope full of cash.

Depending on the facts of the situation, under California law, commercial bribery would be considered a misdemeanor (conviction can result in a jail sentence of a year or less) or a felony (a jail sentence would be more than a year) depending on the value of the kickback.

Is that sale really worth the cost of a criminal defense, the possibility of jail time and the bad publicity and harm to your reputation that could result?

Antitrust Laws

You may think antitrust laws only apply to giant corporations who want to merge, potentially endangering competition. When the federal government blocks these kinds of deals it makes the news. But here's some news for you, antitrust law applies to every business, large and small, and covers a wide array of topics above and beyond which corporation may or may not be able to merge.

Antitrust laws have been enacted by state and federal governments to try to encourage competition and job growth by limiting the control of one or a group of companies of a given market, resulting in artificially high prices and profits. Violations of antitrust laws can result in civil law enforcement lawsuits, lawsuits by individuals and other businesses harmed by the laws being violated and potentially criminal charges. The federal government normally handles antitrust matters involving interstate commerce.

Federal laws are largely made up of the Sherman Act and the Clayton Act while California's version is the Cartwright Act. Federal and state laws are similar in some aspects and different in others.

California's attorney general as well as district attorneys can sue on behalf of the state. The legal action would be to end an unfair practice, punish the party committing the unfair practice by ordering fines or obtain redress for consumers or other businesses being harmed. Criminal charges might also be brought against those accused of violating antitrust laws. Under state law there's also potentially a private right of action which can be filed by competing businesses or consumers to recover for damages suffered as a result of the unfair practice. Victims of antitrust violations can be awarded three times the financial harm done.

Antitrust offenses almost always result in an increase in the prices paid by consumers for goods or services. One company or a group of companies conspiring to violate antitrust laws can also leave law abiding businesses with reduced revenues and higher costs. The impact on the market can vary widely, depending on the type of violation and the market being affected. Consumers might need to pay a dollar or two more for something while a competing business may be forced to close. If the products or services involved are purchased by local or state governments, costs go up so taxes may need to increase or legitimate spending to address other needs might be cut.

There are many practices that could violate state antitrust laws, including,

- Horizontal price-fixing: It would be illegal for business competitors to agree to raise, stabilize or otherwise affect prices. This agreement doesn't have to be in writing or be formalized. An informal understanding between competitors concerning prices would be enough. Specific prices need not be set and any agreement affecting price levels is illegal. A practice of exchanging price information with competitors, if this affects prices, would be illegal. Just attempting to fix prices would be against the law.

- Bid-rigging: This occurs when competitors agree in some way to affect the outcome of competitive bids. This can include submitting identical bids, conspirators agreeing to take turns submitting winning bids, agreements that companies involved they not bid on certain projects or allocating who gets what business.

- Other agreements among competitors: Any agreement among competitors which restrains competition normally violates the law. This includes boycotts (competitors agree not to sell to particular customers or not to buy from particular suppliers), market or customer allocations (competitors agree to whom or where each will sell) and output limitations (agreements to limit quantities marketed, resulting in a lower supply and higher prices) are almost always illegal, regardless of how a company might justify it.

- An agreement between a seller and a buyer over the price, where and to whom the buyer can resell a product could be illegal. Restricting a buyer's freedom to resell products violates antitrust laws if it harms competition more than helping it.

- Tying: A seller requiring a buyer to purchase an unwanted product or service in order to be allowed to purchase what is actually wanted could break the law if the seller has some degree of control over the market for the product or service the buyer wants.

- Monopoly: A business unfairly keeping others from competing with it would be breaking antitrust law. While businesses can compete to obtain and keep customers through ability and efficiency a business with significant market power may not, without legitimate business justification, take actions that exclude or handicap its competitors.

- Mergers: Under federal law, businesses may not merge with or acquire other businesses if the end result would substantially limit competition and result in higher prices. This not only applies to the merger of competing business but also the joining of a supplier and a customer if the market impact is great enough.

- Hiring process: Agreeing with a competitor not to hire away employees from each other or agreeing to limit wages for those in certain positions would violate antitrust law.

Stupid Things That Can Get You in Trouble

There are a number of things you can do to make a bad situation worse. You and your attorney will have enough to do, you don't need to add to your misery, if you've been sued, a government agency is pouring over your records or you think FBI agents may come knocking any day.

If you believe you may be sued over something, first talk to your attorney to discuss what's going on and why you feel that way. That attorney will tell you not to alter or destroy anything that might be used as evidence. That could be tangible items like paperwork or electronic documents like emails, files, text messages or spreadsheets.

Follow the attorney's advice. Don't push the panic button and delete electronic files or shred anything on paper because that would be a really bad idea.

- Your attorney will need all this to investigate what went on and help you establish a defense.

- In a legal proceeding your computers and servers could be searched for deleted documents. Though you thought they were deleted, they may still be accessible.

- In any legal proceeding credibility is key. If magically, out of the blue, relevant evidence on the issue suddenly disappears, the fact finder may see you who you are, a person desperate to cover something up. A copy of an email that you altered won't carry much weight.

- In a civil lawsuit a judge can punish a party severely for tampering with or destroying evidence (even if that occurred prior to the lawsuit being filed), up to a finding of liability against you, so the only issues at a trial are what damages you need to pay and how much.

- Depending on the issue at hand, destruction of evidence may be a crime.

Whether you're being questioned by a government employee, signing documents or making statements, don't lie. Ideally tell the truth and saying nothing is better than telling a lie. One lie will result in more, future lies in order to keep up appearances. The more lies there are the more likely you'll be exposed and the house of cards collapses. Lying under oath is perjury, which could be criminally prosecuted. Once you're caught in a lie your credibility is shot.

Get your attorney involved as soon as you think some government agency is interested in what you're doing or a party that might sue you is asking for information or documents. You need to know about the law and what you divulge, or not, may be critical to protecting your rights. You may want to have your attorney present during any interviews or questioning and your attorney should review documents before they're released.

Social media marketing has become a critical tool for businesses. You may have a Facebook page, a

Twitter account, you're on Instagram and LinkedIn. Your website may have blogs and you might publish press releases.

If you file a lawsuit against another party, or you're the defendant in a lawsuit, understand that the other party's lawyer (or at least a paralegal) will look at all this material. Because credibility is so important in the legal process what you post will be reviewed for inconsistencies with positions or statements made during litigation.

An example is President Trump, who is famous for his high volume of tweets. Over time he has changed past federal policies and instituted new ones that have been challenged in court. Trial and appellate judges have used the contents of his tweets to either delay or strike down his initiatives because his tweets contradict, or can be interpreted as contradicting, what Department of Justice attorneys are arguing on the administration's behalf.

The same might happen to you. If you sue a supplier because their inability to provide you with a key component has severely hurt your business, a press release or Facebook post boasting about what a great year you're having will undercut your claim. Posting photos of a gorgeous new office won't match well with a claim a contractor's many mistakes make your new offices unusable.

We're all guilty of bad judgement at one point or another. If you run a business that bad judgement can have a major impact on your business.

If you're at a point where you think doing something unethical, improper or illegal might be the way to go, stop. When in doubt, don't.

Talk to a lawyer. Discuss the situation. Go over your options and the pros and cons of each. There may be a way to reach your goals without potentially opening you and your business up to liability down the road. This conversation may prevent you and your business from falling down a big, dark hole you might not be able to climb out of.

Mistake No. 6
Be Proactive and Seek Help Early On!

"The best time to engage a business attorney is during the early stage of the deal. If you only seek help after you receive the summons and complaint, it may all be too late." - Tony T. Liu

---

The final legal mistake small business owners make is that they seek help too late. They may believe that attorneys are expensive and not want to incur these expenses.

They hope to save money because they only want to speak with an attorney if they receive a summons and complaint, after they are being sued or when they want to sue somebody else. This is too little too late for a legal consultation because business owners must then pay attorney fees, court costs and litigation costs, which are definitely not cheap (the average litigation cost for small business owners is $91,000 after a lawsuit is initiated.) There is no way around spending money.

"You need an attorney who knows you and your business and can empower your business growth." - Tony T. Liu

There are three types of clients: those who see attorneys as business partners, those who get attorneys involved when they encounter a problem and who those who wait until a lawsuit's been filed. You are better off in the first category because you get a much better return on your investment.

We are not equity business partners but we can be partners in the sense that our advice can empower and help your business grow while we try to ensure that your business does not fall onto a legal and financial land mine and cost you thousands of dollars later on.

These clients retain attorneys very early in their transactions. Business owners may ask their attorneys to attend sales, shareholder, and other key business meetings, so their attorneys have enough background information to advise them about whether or not a transaction is good, bad or something they should put on hold and researched further.

Sometimes attorneys need to understand the transactional background so they can properly advise you. I had a client come to me a few months ago about a very large transaction with a retail giant.

- To fulfill his part of the contractual agreement or obligation, he needed to invest a significant amount of money in capital, equipment, and additional employees to increase his manufacturing capacity so he could fulfill the order with this retailer.

- He calculated the cost and return on investment and found that if he made the investment, he would see a return at the end. It worked out well for him on paper.

- If something happened with the transaction and the retailer did not order any more products from my client, whether it was his fault or not, my client would still be liable for the investment and loan he would need to increase his manufacturing capacity.

- My client needed me to make sure the contract was properly drafted and all the parties' intentions were included in the agreement.

Nothing is guaranteed, but you can minimize the risk of things going wrong. You will have a clear vision as to what to avoid, where to go and where not to go if you get an attorney involved early in the process.

The second group of business owners involve an attorney when they already have a legal issue confronting them.

- If they do not handle the issue properly, it will most likely end up in a lawsuit.

- At that time, they engage attorneys for their legal services and advice about what would happen if they saved the transaction, salvaged the situation, and resolved the issues without going to court.

- They also seek advice about their options and the costs if their case goes to court.

Attorneys may be able to successfully avoid lawsuits by resolving the issues between the parties without the court's intervention through negotiation or mediation, but other times the issues are too large and it's too late for anyone to salvage the business relationship. Things have already been said or done and that particular part of history has been cemented in the timeline.

Attorneys are legal professionals, not time travelers or magicians. We can't change what's already been said or done, but if we were retained early in the process, we may have prevented problems that ended up boiling over.

The third group seeks legal advice when they receive a summons and complaint. If you are in this situation, you typically cannot avoid a lawsuit, and if a lawsuit is filed, unless the parties can reach a settlement you must go through it and obtain a judgment.

When you receive a summons and complaint, the relevant question is, can you successfully defend the case, and if not, how much money do you need to spend to stop the bleeding? Attorneys may not be able to resolve the issues and avoid a lawsuit, but they can advise you about what to do and what your options are in the event a lawsuit occurs.

You need to respond to the summons and complaint within 30 days. If you are the plaintiff, you need the court's intervention to force the other party to do what they promised in the contract. This is the most common situation for my clients.

“You don’t need to be a statistic.”- Tony T. Liu

These are the six legal mistakes that small business owners generally make. If you work on these five areas and develop a strategy for each of these five categories, the risk of a lawsuit is minimized.

In the beginning, I told you that 20 million civil cases are filed in U.S. courts each year, and 60% of these (12 million cases) are breach of contract-related cases, while 75% of the civil cases filed are employment related. I am not sharing these statistics to scare you, but to alert you that if you do not take care of your business, if you are not proactive and do not avoid these types of legal mistakes, you have a high probability of being involved in one of these cases, and if you are, the median cost of each litigation is $91,000, with a starting cost of $54,000.

“Engage a business attorney to guide you on a flat-fee basis, and you can save the money you may have spent on lawsuits and invest it in your business instead.” - Tony T. Liu

---

These costs are on the low end. An initial cost of $54,000 is a reasonable expectation. The median cost of $91,000 is low based on the cases I have handled from beginning to end. I have found that if we are bringing the cases all the way to trial, the cost of that litigation is way beyond $150,000. Now, if the case is settled through mediation or negotiation, the costs were significantly lower. The point is that it is expensive to engage in these kinds of lawsuits.

What happens if you can prevent one lawsuit a year? You will have retained or saved approximately $91,000 each year that you can reinvest into your business to hire employees, purchase equipment, hire consultants, etc. You do not have to become a statistic. You can save yourself money and reinvest the money you saved by avoiding a lawsuit.

The information in this book is for general informational purpose only and does not constitute legal advice. No legal advice is intended. However, if you have a question, call our office and set up an appointment, so we can discuss your situation in detail. Until I receive a phone call, take care of yourself. Invest in your company and yourself, and grow your business.

So How Can I Help You Avoid Fatal Legal Mistakes That May Crush Your Business?

Business owners need to navigate through local, state and federal laws. They must balance staying out of legal trouble while making their operations as profitable as possible. I have been helping business owners achieve these goals since 2003 and I can help your business too through our outside general counsel program.

Lawyers are like doctors. They're necessary but few of us look forward to seeing one. Some of us will only see a doctor only after it's too late and a lot of harm has been done. Annual checkups are missed, tests are skipped and chronic issues become life-threatening emergencies. If you take this kind of approach to the potential legal issues your business faces, that legal heart attack may only be a question of time.

Business owners don't usually seek legal services until they've been sued, suffered harm by another party or they're being investigated by a government agency. This approach of only seeking legal help until after the harm is done wastes huge amounts of time, energy and money. Just as preventative medicine can keep you healthy, preventative legal services can keep your business healthy and thriving.

Would you rather spend your resources on legal issues or focus on running and growing your business?

Smart business owners appreciate the value of being proactive. They understand that preventing or limiting a problem early on can result in substantial savings, whether that problem involves a production line, customer relations or legal issues. After thirteen years of helping businesses put the pieces back together after long simmering legal issues exploded, we are dedicating our practice to serving clients as outside general counsel. We want to help our clients win legal battles before they begin.

You could try to avoid legal landmines yourself, but what will the cost be if your business makes the wrong step? Litigation can be destructive to a business for many reasons.

- Legal costs can be high,
- Management uses up time and energy with the lawsuit (not the business),
- Morale can suffer, and
- A lawsuit could be a public relations nightmare.

By being proactive and using an outside general counsel you may be able to avoid that company heart attack and save the life of your business.

You and your business can save money, time, energy, resources, and most importantly, the heartache and the emotional toll of getting involved in litigation by using our services on a continuous basis, not just after a legal issue has blossomed into a full blown lawsuit or enforcement action by a government agency.

An investment in legal services will pay dividends now and in the future

Businesses that can't afford to hire a general counsel full or part time can afford to hire our services and reap the benefits of a proactive approach to handling legal issues. Your business can receive the benefits of an attorney,

- Who knows you, your management, your business and industry,
- Has thirteen years of experience representing and helping companies like yours,
- Without the costs of a salary and overhead that come with hiring your own general counsel.
-

You can retain our fractional general counsel services for a predictable, value based monthly fee that will make sense for your budget.

Avoid, Minimize, Escape and Conquer

With the help of an outside general counsel your business may be able to avoid legal crises that may otherwise cripple your business. In case a crisis does occur and it can't be resolved, we can also represent your business and defend your legal rights in a cost effective manner because,

- We know your business,
- The preventive measures we've taken should minimize your risk and potential exposure, so
- We will be better prepared to take on a legal challenge, and
- You could escape potential liability and limit your costs.

An entrepreneur can't avoid economic risk but risks of legal problems and the financial harm that can result can be minimized with the help of an outside general counsel. We can help you conquer the legal challenges that stand in the way of your business' success and growth.

Integrity and honor are our core principles

I became a lawyer to help people. I help them run their businesses so they, their families and employees can enjoy better lives. I'm committed to doing the right thing for my clients. I won't do anything that may jeopardize my integrity when I'm working with my clients or opposing parties. I'm not here to over-lawyer issues my clients face, over bill them or create problems where none exists.

It's an honor to represent my clients because they have invested their trust in me and put the future of their businesses in my hands. That's something I take very seriously, not something I take for granted. I work to earn that trust every day.

If you want to learn more about how an outside general counsel can help you and your business, contact our office today at (714) 415-2007.

Who is Tony Liu?

Tony Liu is a business attorney who has been helping Orange County businesses avoid legal problems and address them when they come up for fourteen years. His practice covers a wide range of issues facing the business community including ownership disputes, intellectual property, contract law, commercial real estate and fraud. Tony helps businesses who need an in house general counsel but who would rather have an outside attorney perform that role.

Tony's job is to focus on his clients' legal issues so they can focus on running their businesses. After fourteen years of litigating cases he's learned that even if his client "wins" its case the end result can be destructive and expensive. Tony helps business owners identify and address potential legal issues before they become problems or crises because that's far less costly in time, energy and money for his clients.

Tony is a deal maker, not a deal breaker. He protects his clients while not over-lawyering or making things needlessly complex. Tony speaks the truth to his clients, as difficult as that may be at times, because that's what they need to hear.

In addition to practicing law Tony is a certified success and life coach and he brings that approach to his legal practice. He wants his clients to succeed by preventing legal distractions from draining their energies and resources. Tony empowers his clients through his work and positive, entrepreneurial spirit.

Tony understands business owners would rather invest in their organizations than in their attorneys. He offers a three level service plan which can be paid monthly. Tony's flat fee is a predictable expense that businesses can plan for while avoiding hourly bills that can fluctuate over time. Tony's focus is on being productive and effective, not on billing hours.

Tony has a Bachelor's degree in finance from California State University-Fullerton, a Juris Doctor and a Masters of Law in trial advocacy from the Chapman University School of Law. His office is located in Orange County, California.

Tony can be reached at:

FOCUS LAW - (714) 415-2007

WEBSITE: www.FocusLawLA.com

BLOG: www.orangecountybusinessattorneyblog.com

LINKEDIN: https://www.linkedin.com/in/tony-t-liu-business-trial-attorney-74214bb/

FACEBOOK: https://www.facebook.com/Focus-Law-141950989865721/

Made in the USA
Monee, IL
04 November 2026

67380037R00095